The Lion's Tail

The British Lion or The Master of the World at Home,
Simplicissimus, 1914

The Lion's Tail

An anthology of criticism and abuse

compiled by
Dorothy K. Coveney and
W. N. Medlicott

Nemo bonus Brito est
Ausonius, *Epigr.* 110

CONSTABLE LONDON

First published in Great Britain 1971
by Constable and Company Ltd
10 Orange Street, London WC2

Copyright © 1971 by Dorothy K. Coveney and
W. N. Medlicott

ISBN 0 09 457290 9

PRINTED IN GREAT BRITAIN
BY EBENEZER BAYLIS AND SON LTD
THE TRINITY PRESS, WORCESTER, AND LONDON

Preface

This is not the first time that a collection has been made of extracts abusive of England. Many appeared before and during the two world wars for propaganda and other purposes. They have all been restricted in period, however, and the more widely based anthologies have been devoted to the general foreign view of England, both eulogistic and adverse. But criticism of England has gone on for so long that we felt it might be of interest to compile an anthology which would begin with the first foreign contacts with our island and give a continuous picture of their various and varying anglophobic attitudes down to the present day. This might also throw light on the origin of certain foreign convictions about this country, reveal in some cases how far the criticisms are justified (or at least believed to be so by the critics) and how far merely repetitive, and suggest to what extent the beliefs have influenced the behaviour of other countries towards us at both high and lower levels. This panorama of censure will, we believe, also show how certain traditional complaints have survived long after they have ceased to have any real basis, and perhaps expose some of the motives underlying the abuse.

We are grateful to Dr W. A. Coupe, Dr R. W. Hunt, and Dr Peter Rickard for advice and information on the French and Dutch tailed gibes. Numerous other points we have raised from time to time with colleagues and friends, and for light on these we are indebted to Dr C. J. Bartlett, Mr E. H. Dance, Professor Alun Davies, Professor H. B. Garland, the late Dr R. Koebner, Professor H. I. Nelson, Professor E. H. Phelps

Preface

Brown, and others. We were much helped in our search for material by the facilities we enjoyed at the Institute for Advanced Study, Princeton, N.J., and the Princeton University Library, and in our final quest for missing illustrations we acknowledge gratefully the help of Mr V. J. Riley, of the Institute of Germanic Studies, London, and also of Miss Theo Brown and Miss I. Scott-Elliot, who drove all the way from Devon to Cornwall to photograph the Lanivet cross. Finally we would like to thank Professor Armel Diverres, Mrs Nora Gottlieb, Dr John Henry Jones, Professor E. H. Kossmann, and Miss Audrey Rich for assistance in coping with certain textual problems: for the rest the translations are the work of the editors, unless otherwise acknowledged.

Weybridge, Surrey
January 1971

Dorothy K. Coveney
W. N. Medlicott

Acknowledgements

We would like to thank the following for permission to quote
from copyright material: George Allen & Unwin Ltd *Germany's
Third Empire* by A. Moeller van den Bruck, translated by E. O.
Lorimer, and *Letters from England* by Karel Čapek, translated
by Paul Selver; The Architectural Press Ltd *The Reith Lectures*
by Nikolaus Pevsner; Associated Newspapers Ltd for extracts
from the *Daily Mail* and *The Star*; B. T. Batsford Ltd and
Messrs Daniel C. Joseph *Wars I have seen* by Gertrude Stein;
G. Bell & Sons Ltd *The Life of Napoleon I* by J. H. Rose;
Ernest Benn Ltd *The Memoirs of Paul Kruger* translated by A.
Texeira de Mattos, and *The English: Are they Human?* by G. J.
Renier; The Bodley Head *I Discover the English* by Odette
Keun, *My Discovery of England* by Stephen Leacock, *The Silence
of Colonel Bramble* by André Maurois, and *An Autobiography* by
Jawaharlal Nehru; Jonathan Cape Ltd *Europe* by Count
Hermann Keyserling, and *England's Crisis* by André Siegfried,
translated by H. A. and D. Hemming; Cassell & Company
Ltd *Napoleon at St Helena* by Henri-Gratien Bertrand, ed. by
Paul Fleuriot de Langle and translated by Francis Hume;
Chatto & Windus Ltd *Three Letters on the English* by André
Maurois; the *Chicago Tribune* for extracts from articles between
1927–8; Communist Party of Great Britain *Where is Britain
Going?* by Leon Trotsky; J. M. Dent & Sons Ltd *Mazzini's
Letters* translated by Alice de Rosen Jervis; Deutsche Verlags-
Anstalt *Der Englische Volkscharakter* by Levin L. Schücking;
Dodd, Mead & Company *England: Her Treatment of America* by
G. H. Payne; Doubleday & Company, Inc. *The Goebbels*

Acknowledgements

Diaries translated by Louis P. Lochner; Faber & Faber Ltd and New Directions Publishing Corp. *The Cantos of Ezra Pound* by Ezra Pound; Victor Gollancz Ltd *The Bridegroom Cometh* by Waldo Frank, and *The English Smile* by Christen Hansen; Victor Gollancz Ltd and Simon & Schuster, Inc. *History of the Russian Revolution* by Leon Trotsky, translated by M. Eastman; Hamish Hamilton Ltd *Beware of the English* by W. G. Knop; Hamish Hamilton Ltd and Houghton Mifflin Company *The Simple Art of Murder* by Raymond Chandler; William Heinemann Ltd *Degeneration* by Max S. Nordau, and *The Life and Letters of Walter H. Page* ed. by Burton J. Hendrick; H.M.S.O. *Documents on German Foreign Policy 1918–45* Series D.; Hollis & Carter and the University of Alabama Press *Portrait of Europe* by Salvador de Madariaga; Hutchinson Publishing Group Ltd *Mein Kampf* by Adolf Hitler, translated by J. Murphy, and *Japan must fight Britain* (Hurst & Blackett Ltd) by F. T. Ishimaru, translated by G. V. Rayment; Alfred A. Knopf, Inc. *America Conquers Britain* by Ludwell Denny; Klieber-Verlag, Berlin *Die Blutspur Englands* by Ernst Schultze; Lawrence & Wishart Ltd *V. I. Lenin: British Labour and British Imperialism*; Little, Brown and Company and J. M. Dent & Sons Ltd *The Face is Familiar* by Ogden Nash; Longman Group Ltd *Epistles of Erasmus* translated by F. M. Nichols; Macmillan Company, New York *Breaches of Anglo-American Treaties* by John Bigelow; E. S. Mittler & Sohn G.M.B.H. *Englands Willkür und bisherige Allmacht zur See* by H. Kirchoff; John Murray *A Foreign View of England in the Reign of George I and George II* by Madame van Muyden; Newman Neame Ltd *Meet the British* by Emily Hahn; Oxford University Press and the Royal Institute of International Affairs *The Speeches of Adolf Hitler* translated by Norman H. Baynes; Laurence Pollinger Ltd and Simon & Schuster, Inc. *England Expects every American to Do his Duty* by Quincy Howe; Porter Sargent, Boston *Between Two Wars: the Failure of Education 1920–1940* by Porter Sargent; Routledge & Kegan Paul Ltd *Thus Spake Germany* by W. W. Coole and M. F. Potter, and *Wandering scholar* (Cohen & West) by M. J. Bonn; Secker & Warburg Ltd and Paul R. Reynolds, Inc. *The British* by Drew Middleton; Simon & Schuster, Inc. *With Malice Toward Some*

Acknowledgements

by Margaret Halsey; *The Sunday Times*; The Swedish Institute for Cultural Relations *Impressions of England 1809-10* by Erik Geijer, translated by E. Sprigge and C. Napier; The Sydney *Sun*; *The Times*; Verlag Ullstein G.M.B.H. 'Das Englische Volk und die Kultur' by M. Frischeisen-Köhler in *Das Englische Gesicht*; *The Washington Post* for extracts by Fred Hechinger, Henry La Mont, and Drew Pearson; John Baker Publishers Ltd *The Reflections of a Russian Statesman* by K. P. Pobyedonostseff; Albert Bonniers Förlag *Från det moderna England* by Gustaf F. Steffen.

We regret that we have been unable to trace the copyright owners of the following works and we would be grateful for any information which would enable us to apply for formal permission and acknowledge it in a future edition; G. B. Adams *Why Americans Dislike England*; Ewald Banse *Germany Prepare for War!*, translated by Alan Harris; Henri Béraud *Faut-il reduire l'Angleterre en esclavage?*, Sarah Bernhardt *My Double Life*; Stella Dean, letter in *The Times* 1953; C. N. J. Du Plessis *The Transvaal Boer speaking for Himself*; Alfred Geiser *Das perfide Albion*; J. Just Lloret *Inglaterra, arbitra de España*; J. P. Oliveira Martins *The England of Today*, translated by C. J. Willdey; Carl F. H. Peters *England and the English*; Alexander Tille *Aus Englands Flegeljahren*; A. P. F. von Tirpitz *Der Aufbau der deutschen Weltmacht*; *Tolstoi on Shakespeare* ed. V. G. Tchertkoff; Admiral zu der Valois *Nieder mit England*; General B. Viljoen *My Reminiscences of the Anglo-Boer War*; Lin Yutang *Between Tears and Laughter*.

The frontispiece and plates V, X, XI and XII are reproduced by courtesy of the Institute of Germanic Studies, University of London; plate I by courtesy of the Freunde der Kunsthalle, Hamburg; plate II from an original photograph kindly supplied by Miss Theo Brown; plate III by courtesy of the Bayrische Staatsbibliothek, Munich, and plates IV, VI, VII, VIII and IX by courtesy of the Trustees of the British Museum, London.

Contents

Illustrations

Introduction

Rous'd by the lash of his own stubborn tail,
Our lion now will foreign foes assail.
>   Dryden, *Astraea Redux*, I, 117.

A lion so with self-provoking smart
(His rebel tail scourging his nobler part)
Calls up his courage, then begins to roar
And charge his foes, who thought him mad before.
>   Waller, *To my Lord of Falkland*, 37-40.

Twisting the lion's tail has been a popular sport with foreigners throughout the ages, although the expression seems to have been invented by the British themselves. The British emblem was frequently referred to as a leopard (or leopards), and the tails were, at least at first, attached individually to the English rather than nationally.

But tweaking and twisting the lion's tail has not been a foreign monopoly: self-criticism by the islanders has at times almost outdone foreign efforts and may have done much to keep the sport alive, and there is a theory that, with his perverted sense of humour, the Englishman is actually amused at the gibes. Ralph Lombardi, an American, said, 'I am not aware of another nation of people who permit and invite criticism and enjoy laughing at themselves as much as the English do'; similarly André Maurois, 'There is no nation which stands criticism, even severe criticism, so well as the English'; and

H. G. Wells, in *Mr Britling Sees it Through*, 'That favourite topic of all intellectual Englishmen, the adverse criticism of things British'. As early as 1663 de Sorbière had commented in his *Voyage en Angleterre*, 'They take pleasure in having the truth told and the character of the people has been more than once printed at London and that writ by a native who hath not spared either reproof or censure'. That the Englishman sincerely believes in his faults is often doubted: André Siegfried calls self-criticism a 'very English affectation', and Mr Harold Macmillan, at the 1961 Royal Academy Dinner, declared that 'we are masters of denigration, but all the time we do it with our tongue in our cheek. It is part of our tradition.' At any rate, the sport became so popular that certain Britons decided it was a money-spinner and began joining in the fun under foreign names (e.g. John Shebbeare as B. Angeloni, 1755, Horace Walpole as 'Xo Ho, a Chinese philosopher', 1757, Goldsmith with his 'Chinese' letters, 1762, Robert Southey as 'Don Manuel Alvarez Espriella', 1807, and the anonymous Englishman who posed as the Chinaman 'Wo Chang', 1897) until finally self-castigation became even more the rage and foreigners issued anti-British publications under British *noms de guerre* (Paul Blouet as Max O'Rell, 1883).

Criticism of the British by the British for the British would make an interesting anthology in itself, but the present small volume is confined to the foreign view of Albion, from Cicero in 53 B.C. to present times. Although representative, it is of necessity only a sample: in the French Revolution era alone collections of anti-British pamphlets amount to many large volumes, and during certain more recent periods of tension, foreign newspapers and wireless programmes have added almost daily to the bulk of verbal tail-twisting. It is hardly necessary to add that the anthology starts by being more or less comprehensive, and becomes more and more selective as the centuries progress.

The lion as the British emblem obviously has its origin in the Royal coat-of-arms. When Henry I of England knighted his son-in-law Geoffrey Plantagenet, Count of Anjou, he presented him with a shield bearing golden lions, and arms with two lions (the arms of the Duchy of Normandy) are said to

1 The Curtailing of St Thomas Becket's Sumpter-Mule, altar-piece
by Meister Francke, Kunsthalle, Hamburg

2 Tailed man on cross in churchyard at Lanivet, Cornwall

have been borne by the first four Norman kings. But it was not until about 1189 that a shield bearing three lions became the recognized arms of the English kings, the third lion being added for either mystical or historical reasons, apparently unrecorded.

Not that at that time they were always known as lions. The true lion was shown side-face, erect and rampant, open-jawed, with extended claws and lashing tail, in characteristic leonine ferocity; when the same beast was shown stealthily advancing to the attack, with three feet on the ground and one paw raised, its face turned to the spectator (passant guardant), it was known as a leo-pardé ('lion as a pard') or leopard. In other words early heralds, having probably seen neither animal in the flesh, distinguished them by their attitudes rather than their spots. The simple device of three golden leopards on a red field was thus borne by Richard I, John, Henry III, and the three Edwards until 1340, and as late as the reign of Edward III the royal crest was described as a leopard, and Henry V appointed a Leopard Herald. But owing to the great popularity of the lion as a charge, both for the arms of the English nobility, as well as on the Continent, and in so many attitudes, the appellation 'lion' tended to oust 'leopard', even when it showed the leopard stance. As early as the fourteenth century the chief herald of Scotland was known as the Lyon King of Arms (*leo rex armorum*) — still today Lord Lyon King of Arms — and heraldically it was finally established, in England at any rate, that the lion passant guardant (formerly leopard) should be blazoned as the 'lion of England'.[1] Thus the King of Beasts, which had never been spotted anyway, finally came into its own in heraldry, although when Napoleon declared he would drive the English leopards into the sea, he was not only denying them leonine courage but proving that the heraldic confusion had after all survived, at least in denigration. From the lion of England to the lion-as-England is a step of natural development, a symbol seemingly invented by the British themselves and first used by Dryden in 1660, as far as can be traced.

The tail is older, and plural. From early medieval times the

[1] E. E. Dorling, *Leopards of England* (1913).

English were said to have tails, and 'tailed English' (*angli caudati, anglois coué*) was a frequent term of abuse, particularly in France.[1] Its origin is obscure. The earliest known reference is found in the *Isengrimus* of Nivardus of Ghent (*c.* 1150), 'Non habet hic caudem, velut Anglicus alter habebat'. The phrase also appears in a Continental Latin document of about 1163, and Richard of Devizes, in his account of the crusade of Richard I (1190), mentions that amongst the crusaders in Messina 'caudati' was a taunt specifically applied to the English ('Anglos et caudatos nominabant'). That it was current in France in the twelfth century is clear from the use of the word *coütz* (*coué*) by the Provençal poet Peire d'Auvergne in a poem written some time between 1158 and 1180. In England itself, however, there was already a legend of tailed Englishmen. Gocelin's life of St Augustine, written about 1080–90, records that the inhabitants of a Dorset town made fun of the saint by attaching fishtails to his garments, and the incident appears again in William of Malmesbury's *Gesta Pontificum Anglorum* (1143), although with no mention as yet of any deserved or undeserved consequences. The Anglo-Norman poet Wace, however, in his *Brut* in 1155, relates the story and adds that, as a punishment for the insult, the inhabitants of the town and their descendants all have tails. In some manuscripts the town is given as Rochester, instead of Dorchester, possibly owing to its proximity to Canterbury, a town more readily associated with St Augustine. In the thirteenth century the Old English *Brut* of Layamon expands Wace's account, declaring that 'the whole race was shamed, for muggles [tails] they had, and in all company they are called mugglings'. At all events, the scene of the crime became established in popular tradition as Rochester (or Strood near Rochester) and a thirteenth-century Latin satire, composed in France and contained in a fourteenth-century manuscript in the Bibliothèque Nationale, not only attacks the inhabitants of Rochester for their treatment of St Augustine and their treachery, but accuses the English generally of untrustworthiness; on this occasion the Scots and Welsh are specifically excluded.

[1] P. Rickard, '*Anglois coué* and *l'Anglois qui couve*', *French Studies* VII (1953), p. 48 ff.

In some continental countries, however, it was held that the curtailing of St Thomas Becket's sumpter-mule was the cause of the Kentish deformity. Becket's biographer, William Fitzstephen, tells how, on Christmas Eve in 1170, five days before the murder of St Thomas, Robert de Broc sent his nephew to lie in wait for Becket, and cut off the tails of his mule and one of his horses. St Thomas alluded to the insult in his sermon on Christmas Day and at his final meeting with his murderers, and excommunicated de Broc. That this was known in Germany is borne out by the early fifteenth-century altarpiece of Meister Francke (see Plate 1).

Mention might be made here of a third local legend of tails in England, which may or may not have been known on the Continent and therefore cannot be said definitely to have strengthened the belief in the English *caudati*. Visitors to Devon occasionally hear it said that the Cornish detach their tails before crossing the Tamar, hanging them up in Saltash town hall until their return. Another favourite but less frequent report is that Cornish dockers crossing the ferry to work in Devonport leave their tails on the Tail Stone at Tor Point[1] and receive a ticket for them, so as to be able to reclaim them on the return journey.[2] Unlike the Dorset and Kent legends, the Cornish tails seem unrecorded in documents, achieving mention only in Baring Gould's *Red Spider* and in his *Curious Myths of the Middle Ages*. In spite of Baring Gould's assertion of medieval origin, the lack of documentary evidence makes it impossible to suggest when the legend arose. Nor do we know whether, like the Dorset and Kent legends, it became associated with an insult to a saint. Robert Hunt, in his *Popular Romances of the West of England*, alludes to the tradition that the Lizard people used to go on all fours, but gives no date or period of this supposed belief. There are, however, in Cornwall, two early crosses,[3] one in Penzance and the other in the churchyard at Lanivet, which bear carvings of tailed men (see Plate 2). The Penzance Cross was originally the Market Cross, and certainly stood in the middle of the market place in 1836.

---

[1] This stone has now either been removed, or is no longer known by this name.
[2] T. F. G. and H. Dexter, *Cornish Crosses, Christian and Pagan*, 1938, p. 46.
[3] Dexter, pp. 41–4.

Later it was moved to a side wall, and part was chipped away to fit it to the site. It was subsequently moved to the Morrab Gardens, and now stands in the Penlee Memorial Gardens.[1] The Lanivet cross is to be found on the north side of the circular churchyard. It would be exceedingly interesting if these crosses could be accurately dated. Lettering on the Penzance stone, difficult to decipher because of its rubbed state, suggests that the script cannot be earlier than the ninth century, but there is no certainty that the cross does not antedate the inscription. Nor is it possible to say whether the little tailed men on the two crosses represent tailed Cornishmen. But they are certainly figures with tails, both with their feet turned to the right in order to show the tail, which has a thickening at the end, rather like the tuft on a lion's tail, but possibly symbolic. The Penlee man appears to have something like a whip in his right hand, but it is difficult to be sure. There is also a Cornish custom called 'tail-piping': on 1 April, strictly after 12 noon, when the April Fool's jokes are at an end, the boys are said to go round hanging paper tails on passers-by. No one seems to know whether this has any connection with the Cornish legend of tailed men.

The late Dr Dexter alluded to the existence of yet another tailed figure on a monolithic slab-cross in Wales, known best as the Maen Achwynfan cross, near Whitford in Flintshire. The late Dr Nash-Williams, on the other hand, suggested, although with some uncertainty, that it was an ithyphallic figure.[2] It would be difficult to insist that the appendage is in fact a tail. There remains, however, the mystery of two figures on the pillar-stone in the rectory at Llanhamlach in Breconshire.[3] These, one male and one female, wear long straight tunics, and both have an appendage showing below. If these are not meant to be tails, it is difficult to see what they are. Yet according to Welsh historians so far consulted, no legend of tailed men can be tracked down in Wales, nor references to the tailed English.

[1] We are indebted to Mr J. Beckerlegge, of Mousehole, for drawing our attention to the whereabouts of this cross.
[2] V. E. Nash-Williams, *The Early Christian Monuments of Wales* (1950) Plate LXXI, 12.
[3] *ibid.* Plate LIII, 61.

A theory put forward by Dr Enklaar[1] (who is apparently not familiar with the Cornish legend) that the first representations of tailed Englishmen are to be found in the top border of the Bayeux Tapestry, just to the right of the Turold incident, is hardly tenable, as they are usually taken to be female centaurs. The little man being pursued by the Normans in the final rout of the English at the very end of the tapestry, however, is holding up in his right hand something which could well be his tail. If so, this is the first appearance in history of the English *caudati*.

From the thirteenth century the tail began to be looked upon as a peculiarly English appendage.[2] In 1217 the Chronicle of Lanercost speaks of Louis of France, though defeated at Lincoln, as breaking the English tails (*quia caudas fregit eorum*), and Jacques de Vitry records towards the middle of the century that French students called the English 'potatores et caudatos' ('boozers and tailed'). Matthew Paris, the St Albans Chronicler, likewise alluded to the English soldiers as *caudati* (1250). By this time, too, the English had produced their own term, 'taylards'. The thirteenth-century English poem *Richard Coeur de Lion*, allegedly a version of a French romance, has the lines:

Out, taylards, of my paleys!
Now go and say your tayled king
That I owe him no thing.

The Scots early joined in the chorus of abuse. In 1217 a Scottish satirist referred to members of an English church mission as 'caudati'; at the attack on Dunbar in 1296 the castle garrison loudly railed at the English as 'canes caudatos' (tailed dogs), and the night before the battle of Dupplin Moor (1332) the Scottish soldiers retired for the night singing loud songs about tailed Englishmen. The failure of the siege of Dunbar Castle in 1338 evoked the remark in an anonymous Latin poem 'the tails came in and had their day', and tailed insults continued to be hurled south across the Scottish border until the sixteenth century, when John Skelton and George

---

[1] Th. Enklaar, 'De gestaarte Engelsman', *Koninkl. Nederl. Akad. v. Wetensch.*, *Afd. Letterkunde*, Deel 18 (1955), no. 5.
[2] G. Neilson, *Caudatus Anglicus, A Mediaeval Slander* (1896) is still the most comprehensive account of the gibe.

Dundas had their well-known fish-market exchange of invective (see below, Section I).

The gibe appears most frequently, however, in medieval France, and mention can be made here of only a few more examples. In a *pièce farcie* of mixed Latin and French by the monk of Silly in the thirteenth century the English are likened to scorpions and hence tailed (*scorpionibus similes, Por ce sont dit Anglois coué*), and a late fourteenth-century poem of Eustache Deschamps ends with the refrain, 'Lift up your tails, lift them up' (*Levez votre queue, levez*). In 1429 a poem beginning 'Arière, Englois couez, arière!' was sung as the French hymn of hate by Joan of Arc's troops (see Section I). In 1436 de Monstrelet records in his *Chronique* that Parisians shouted 'à la keuwe!' ('after the tails'), and according to Jean Chartier's Chronicle of Charles VII, citizens of the French capital also shouted 'au regnard!' ('after the fox'). Later in the same century (1477) Jean Molinet declares that cats owe their tails to their English origin: 'This nun cat comes from Calais . . . it must be of English origin as it has a very long tail.'[1] Although abuse of England in France does not diminish in the sixteenth century, the '*coué*' gibe tends to give way to other, equally strong, invective, particularly as it is in this century that the taunt of English 'perfidy' begins to be frequent. But the gibe lives on in references to the English as wolves, foxes, dragons, serpents and crocodiles.

Accused also on the Continent of being 'mighty swearers', or 'goddams', the English became known as tailed goddams, and thus 'godons coués' was a recognized synonym in France for 'English'. Another proverbial saying, 'saoul comme un Anglois' ('drunk as an Englishman') was frequently coupled with the epithet 'tailed', and 'godons pourceaux remplis de bière', and 'angli caudati, qui sunt ad pocula nati', are further examples of the scurrilous and vulgar abuse aimed at the English by the French and Germans in the Middle Ages. Other examples will be found in Section I.

Before leaving the medieval period we must mention another taunt similar to *coué* and perhaps even a derivative of

---

[1] Neilson, *op. cit.* p. 458, mistranslates the first line 'Ce cat nonne vient des Callés' as 'This cat comes *not* from Calais', but the remainder of the poem makes it clear that it is a 'nun cat', although the allusion, probably political, is obscure.

it.[1] From the thirteenth century the English were also associated with *couvé*, and were derided as sitting on eggs and 'hatching' them. The meaning seems later to have further developed to 'brooding' or 'scheming', particularly in the political sphere. But the hatching taunt survives until the twentieth century and was revived for propaganda purposes in the second world war (see Plate 3).

In the fifteenth and sixteenth centuries the English continued to play their part in the perpetuation of the 'tailed' legend. Although the Augustine insult does not appear in the original *Legenda Aurea*, the English *Golden Legend* (1483) includes the incident in the life of St Augustine, and whereas Fordun's *Scotichronicon* omits it, Bower's fifteenth-century version mentions both the attaching of fishtails to St Augustine's garments and the docking of Becket's horse. The two legends are at last combined, the Augustine incident being located in Dorset (the town taking the name of Muglington) and the Becket incident at Rochester. In the sixteenth century Hector Boece, in his Chronicles of Scotland, suppressed the Augustine story, but his translator John Bellenden[2] again lays the scene in Dorset, naming the town as Miglintoun. No town of that name has so far been identified. But gradually Kent becomes the favourite home of the legend, and some foreigners like Polydore Vergil (*Historia Anglica*, 1534) continue to cite only the Becket version.

But in spite of the fact that the English were almost as much to blame as the Continentals for keeping the legend alive, a few Englishmen in the sixteenth and seventeenth centuries were stung to refute it. Vehement denials of the tails appear in the works of John Bale, William Lambarde, and Thomas Fuller. John Bale (1546) blames the Catholics, saying that 'Englande hath in all other landes a perpetual dyffamy of tayles by their wrytten legendes of lyes', and Lambarde, with misplaced zeal and inaccuracy, puts the blame on Polydore

---

[1] P. Rickard, '*Anglois coué* and *l'Anglois qui couve*', *French Studies* VII (1953), p. 51. Dr Rickard points out that in medieval French *u* and *v* would be written alike, and *coué* could mean *coué* or *couvé*: thus the hatching idea might have been invented by someone not yet familiar with the legend of tailed Englishmen.

[2] In the Bellenden MS at University College, London (MS. Angl. 1), however, the reference to the tails has been crossed out by a later hand.

Vergil for transferring the Augustine story to St Thomas Becket, calling him 'a covetous gatherer of lying Fables'. (To be fair to Polydore Vergil, he only imputes tails to the descendants of the perpetrators of the deed in Strood, and asserts that the tailed men had now died out.) Fuller, in 1655, repeats Bale's denials. Nevertheless two years earlier the inevitable English opposition to the denials appeared in the person of John Bulwer, who, in his *Anthropometamorphosis* (1650) declared his belief in the tails, citing the Becket story. He mentions tails seen by Cromwell's troops in Ireland. From the seventeenth century onwards there are many instances of the term 'Kentish Long-Tayles' (e.g. *Robin Good-fellow, His Mad Prankes, 1628*) which now begins to apply to inhabitants of all Kent, instead of merely Strood or Rochester. The best-known quotation is perhaps Andrew Marvell's line, 'For Becket's sake, Kent always shall have tails' (*The Loyal Scot*, 1.95).

A generation later, in the middle of the century, the theme harped on so long by the French is taken up full blast by the Netherlands. The Anglo-Dutch War of 1652–4, a culmination of fierce naval and trade rivalry, produced a spate of anti-English verse and cartoons, in which the Englishman figures as the 'Startman' (variously spelt 'staert-' or 'staart-'), or 'tail-man'. As Cromwell was obviously the main target of Dutch hate, a cartoon of 1658 labels him as 'Den afgrysselikken Start-man' or 'the Horrible Tail-Man' (see Plate 4). He is shown with a long, fat, coin-encrusted tail, which various people are trying to attack: the Zeelander has caught it in a grappling-iron, and is apparently prising off the coins, the Dutchman appears to be twisting it, the Scotsman hacking off the tip, held by a Royalist, while a Frisian and an Irishman with a knife are hurrying to the fray. With his back turned to all this, Cromwell is refusing the three British crowns offered by Fairfax, watched by Admiral Black (i.e. Blake) and some members of Parliament. A bulldog, symbolizing the English people, is being kept quiet with a bone. The small inset cartoon shows the plunder unloaded from English ships being sold on the quayside.

The Dutch word for England, 'Engelandt' or 'Engellandt' (similar to the poetical German form, 'Engelland'), with its obvious alternative interpretation of 'Angel-land', was a ready-made pun which the satirists seized upon with monotonous persistence. They refer to the English as 'engelen mit starten' ('tailed angels'), then in the singular as 'den zwarten engel' ('the black, or fallen, angel'), and finally quite bluntly as 'diuvelen' ('devils'). 'Hoe krijght dat Duyvel-rijck de naam van Engel-landt?' is of course not original—the old Hanseatic saying, 'England, land of shame, how come you, land of Satan, to the name of Angel-land?', antedates it. But the Dutch make it their own, and many variants of the 'tailed man, tailed angel, black angel, devil' theme are to be found in the patriotic poems of the 1650s–1670s (*see* Section I). Several Dutch cartoons of this period show Britain as a bulldog, or a nation of individual dogs, one of the best-known, perhaps, being the 'Leeuw en hondengeveght' ('lion-and-dog fight') of 1652, the lion in this case symbolizing Flanders. Cromwell is egged on by two dogs, the tails of which a Dutch sailor is trying to nip off with red-hot tongs. A variation on the 'tailed angel' or 'devil' motif is to refer to the English as curs, although one couplet, from a poem of 1653 on Van Galen's victory at Livorno ('If you call yourselves soldiers, do not hold your tails between your legs like panic-stricken dogs'), seems very much like an echo of the late fourteenth-century French refrain already referred to, 'Lift up your tails, lift them up!', doubtless a taunt of cowardice. References to other animals appear too, as already noted in France, amongst them scorpions and griffins.[1]

Did foreigners really believe in the tails? Many English soldiers fought and fell on foreign soil, corpses were robbed and must have been seen to be tailless. Writers like Froissart, who spent many years in England, do not allude to the subject at all. It was poets like Eustache Deschamps, who in his youth had seen the English invasion of 1358, the march on Chartres, and the signing of the Treaty of Bretigny, who bitterly taunted the invading troops with refrains such as 'Lift up your tails'. The origin of these exclusively English tails remains a mystery, and could even, as has happened with other abuse, be

[1] For an account of the Dutch gibes, see Th. Enklaar, 'De gestaarte Engelsman', *loc. cit.*

an English invention. It is easier to guess why the idea caught on and remained attached for so long. Ridicule of an enemy as something sub-human, akin to curs, serpents, vipers, dragons, even crocodiles, and devilish to boot, is not confined to one period of history or to one victim: but when it could all be summed up in one neat ready-made catch-phrase as forceful and suggestive as *coué*, particularly in the combination *godons coués*, it was too good a cliché to drop.

As has been seen, the Dutch made great play with the gibe until the 1670s, when the insults died down with the marriage of William of Orange and Mary. It may be a pure coincidence that it was almost precisely at this time that Dryden uses the term 'British Lyon' for England, and speaks of the lash of his mighty tail, and the lion, constantly referred to by subsequent British writers, becomes the recognized synonym for Britain (or England, as foreigners use these terms indiscriminately). Bismarck's remark, in a letter to Leopold von Gerlach in 1857, that 'an islander is an easily caught animal, especially the Englishman with his long tail of national arrogance and ignorance', makes no reference to the lion, but gives the tail a national significance. It is difficult to pinpoint the origin of the expression 'twisting the lion's tail', so often used by journalists, but it was certainly current in Canada in the late 1880s, and seems to have been especially associated at that time with Irish influence in the United States.[1] It too was possibly a British invention. But however recent the expression, the sport has been popular for so many centuries that, before discussing the many faults of which England has been accused, it might set the accusations in perspective to recall the highlights of anglophobia abroad.

There seems to have been little expression of genuine hatred of Britain in the Dark and Middle Ages. Her enemies, the Saxons, Danes and Normans came, saw, and conquered, and thereafter became 'English'. In 1160 or thereabouts Pierre Riga says that the English cannot be trusted, the Austrian Otto de Sancto Blasio is rude about them after the fall of Acre in 1191, and

[1] Cf. D. G. Creighton, *John A. Macdonald, the Old Chieftain* (1955), p. 508.

early in the next century the Welshman, Giraldus Cambrensis, calls the English the 'most degraded of all the races under Heaven'. But such early criticism is rare, and it is perhaps to be expected that the French, the first enemy who failed to conquer them, should also be the first real England-haters and -baiters, and that, during the Hundred Years War, as their wrath increased, their language should become more and more vituperative. At the end of Edward III's reign (about 1375) in a Latin 'Dispute between an Englishman and a Frenchman' the English are called 'dregs of mankind, shame of the world and the absolute end' (*faex hominum, pudor orbis et ultima rerum*). In the same century Eustache Deschamps prophesies that England will be so destroyed that no trace will remain, and that one day visitors to the site will point and say, 'Here was England'—the first, it might be added, of many such prophecies.

But anglophobia in France did not lessen with the ending of the Hundred Years War in 1453. The English still held Calais and it is clear, from the constant cries of 'Go away, you English' ('Videz, Anglais, hors de nos terres', 'Allez-vous-en musser', 'Retirez-vous arrière') followed by suitable invective, that it was the presence of English soldiers that irked them most at this time. But the volleys of abuse waxed and waned with political events: after a violent spate in the early sixteenth century the marriage of Henry VIII's sister Mary with Louis XII brought a brief lull, although in the 1520s hate poems were again numerous, mostly with accusations of treachery and untrustworthiness. There was fierce French reaction to the divorce of Henry and Catherine, and to the executions of Sir Thomas More and Anne Boleyn, and then a lessening of abuse in 1558 when Calais was, for the first time in 200 years, freed from the English, and Mary Stuart was married to the Dauphin. Protestants and Huguenots hoped for English support, although the execution of Mary shocked the Continent deeply, and it is interesting to note that much of the French criticism, both in verse and pamphlet form, was in fact written by disgruntled English and Irish Catholic refugees, and published in French translation. After the defeat of the Armada, England's prestige rose, and this, combined with increasing regard for Elizabeth and growing fear of Spain, more or less silenced the criticism, and James I's accession was marred by no violent outbursts from the French.

With Spain the open breach came only in 1585, but it followed a quarter of a century of tension. Since the days of Henry VII the Spanish ambassadors had been disliked for their haughty airs, and their reports leave no doubt that they felt that there was every justification for their sense of superiority. Personal contacts between the two countries were few outside court circles, but the English developed a fierce animosity nourished by the sufferings of sailors at the hands of the Inquisition, and the Spanish denounced as robbers and pirates the plunderers of their colonies and treasure ships.

The milder attitude of many continentals during the later years of Elizabeth's reign was not due only to the comparative absence of provocation on the part of the English. Whereas their national characteristics had been mainly judged hitherto by the behaviour of their troops on foreign soil, foreigners now began to visit England more frequently and see for themselves. Earlier visitors had been sparse: noteworthy in the fifteenth century perhaps, only the Bohemian Count Rozmital, Erasmus on the first of his six visits, and the earliest of the Venetian ambassadors who reported on England critically to the Doge. We have several accounts by these latter, spread over the first half of the sixteenth century, and one lone account by a visiting Greek, Nicander Nucius, two years before the death of Henry VIII. Edward VI's reign saw an influx of visiting scholars, but most of them seem to have been too busy to pass judgement on their hosts, and the Venetian accounts ceased abruptly when Elizabeth, at her succession in 1558, severed diplomatic relations with Venice. But her brilliant court drew many other foreigners, amongst them the Dutchmen, Levinus Lemnius and Van Meteren, and Rathgeb, the Secretary to the Duke of Würtemberg. Born in London of Tuscan parents, Giovanni (or John) Florio doubtfully counts as a foreigner, but his 'England is the paradise of women, the purgatory of men, and the hell of horses', so often quoted about his adopted country, has been included nevertheless. None of these visitors was particularly venomous, and it seems significant that the Italian J. C. Scaliger, who wrote of the 'perfidious, haughty,

savage, disdainful, stupid, mad, slothful, inhospitable, inhuman English', never saw England as far as we know.

With James's accession in 1603 the Venetian ambassadors
returned to London and the Duc de Sully came to congratulate
the new monarch. Continental Catholics approved of Mary
Stuart's son and Anglo-French relations seemed set fair.
Charles's marriage with Henrietta Maria, however, which
should have fostered greater French cordiality, brought its own
frictions, and the La Rochelle affair (1627–8) inspired new abuse
and revived traditional sayings. Buckingham, who supported
the rebels, earned particular censure and was derided as a
'lascivious goat of haughty Albion', and Massoni's 'From
England comes neither a good wind nor a good war' appears
again in a poem of Ménipée de Francion. With Buckingham's
assassination and the new peace with France, criticism is less
vocal, although St Amant, in his poem *L'Albion* (1644) revives
old hates and the 'tailed' gibe, and prays that the barbaric
island may be sunk in the sea. But the isolated taunts became a
thundering chorus on the execution of Charles I, which
horrified the Continent: the English are crazy, cruel, demons,
wolves, and traitors. In poem after poem occur the words
'maudits, cruels et forcenés', and it is at this time that the term
'perfidious', already used of the English in earlier centuries, is
heard more and more frequently. (The use of the 'Perfidious
Albion' slogan will be dealt with later.) Cromwell enjoyed, it is
true, a certain respect in France, although they could not
forgive him his crime against the King, but with Anglo-Dutch
rivalry and the war of 1652–4 he became the butt of Dutch
satire, as has been seen in the account of the 'tailed' gibes.

Thus throughout the Stuart period the French blew hot and
cold, although it was the heat that was anti-British. The
Restoration in 1660 was hailed in France, particularly by the
Catholics, who, disappointed that Charles II did little for their
faith, pinned their hopes on James II, until he himself was
forced to take refuge amongst them in 1688. The French had
sympathized over the Great Fire of London in the '60s, but
looked upon it as God's judgement on the English for their
'insupportable arrogance' and regicide. But all this was long-
distance criticism: travellers to England during this period

were comparatively few—the thousands who flocked thither after the revocation of the Edict of Nantes in 1685 would hardly write disparagingly of England for the benefit of France —and it is perhaps significant that those who came to see the country, such as Coulon, de Sorbière, and Misson de Valbourg, admitted that the English were lazy, gluttonous, arrogant and uncivil to foreigners, but reported on them kindly otherwise. Misson, one of the refugees, declared that the 'more strangers are acquainted with the English, the more they will esteem and love them'.

With the accession of William and Mary, vilification of England died down in the Netherlands, and Germans, who had crossed the Channel little except during the latter part of Elizabeth's reign, began to include England in their grand tour. But their accounts were not particularly vicious; and the Swiss Louis de Muralt, whose *Lettres sur les Anglois* were much read on the Continent, accused the English of corruption and debauchery (wine, women and dice), sloth and credulity, but found much to praise.

With the establishment of the Hanoverians on the British throne, it was to be expected that at least the Germans would be moderately anglophile, but oddly enough it was a Frenchman, Voltaire, who, after his visit of 1726–9, sold England not only to France but also to most of the Continent, with a resulting burst of anglomania never enjoyed since. In no other period of history, surely, would Frenchmen be found trying their best to look English, with horses, jockeys, English dress-coats and top-boots! Hence at least the first half of the eighteenth century contributes little to this anthology. Not that the travellers who came in abundance were completely uncritical. The social liberty they so much admired led, they believed, to such concomitant abuses as licentiousness, debauchery, and savagery; the cruelty of the English, after centuries of regicide and a national drama full of 'bloody deeds', still prompted them, as Voltaire later related in *Candide* (1759) to 'kill an admiral now and then to encourage the others' (a reference to the execution of Admiral Byng), and to 'take a stern delight in slaughtering men with the pretended sword of the law' (1764). Cock-fighting, bull-baiting, and public hangings were favourite spectacles. Voltaire denied the British any great aptitude for painting or music, or indeed any gift for tragedy (he finds *Hamlet* a 'gross and barbarous play') and their arrogance, national pride, melancholy, and taciturnity were bywords. But in spite of such strictures, most of which were not new, and many of which were deserved, anglomania was the fashion in Europe until after the middle of the century.

The Seven Years War (1756–63), as might have been expected, worsened England's relations with her enemies, France, Austria, and Russia; more surprisingly it had an equally bad effect on her ally Prussia, who resented the partial abandonment of her interests after 1761. Frederick accused the British government of breaking faith with its allies, and revived the taunt of 'perfidy', used now in a different sense, and with definite propagandist aim. The American War of Independence (1776–83) was opportune for reinforcing Frederick's hate campaign, although the most vocal critic in America was Thomas Paine, who, in spite of all temptation, remained an Englishman. He speaks of her treachery ('[England's] character is gone and we have seen the funeral'), and declares that her idea of national honour is 'to threaten with the rudeness of the bear, and to devour with the ferocity of a lion'. Britain's decline in prestige on the loss of the American colonies helped further to fan the anglophobic flame, and it now only needed the French Revolution to bring to white heat the fires of hate, leaving embers in many parts of Europe which have never since quite died out. It was not a burst of spontaneous anti-British feeling, but a deliberate campaign by Robespierre to foster and intensify hate against not only the British government, but also the English people, or, as he himself worded it in 1794, 'animer de plus en plus votre haine contre les Anglais', and as Paul Gauran, in the Corps Législatif in 1798 termed it, 'nationalizing hate against England'. A note at the end of Bertrand Barère's *La Liberté des Mers* (1798) declares it was composed 'dans le seul objet de nationaliser, avec force, la haine des républicains contre l'infâme gouvernement anglais'. It was an organized attempt to stamp out any remaining traces of anglomania which might have survived in Europe from earlier decades, and to what extent it succeeded as propaganda was not even guessed at by its perpetrators, who could never have envisaged the legacy they would hand down to twentieth-century Europe. The immediate result was a spate of anti-English literature, speeches, pamphlets, operas, plays, and poems, much of it emanating from the early years of the nineteenth century, just before Napoleon became Emperor. The forceful 25-stanza hymn of hate, *Ode aux Français* (1804), containing all the clichés and prophesying England's downfall, is a fair example of these tirades. Napoleon continued the campaign, although the gibe most frequently associated with his name was not in fact his own invention.

The German attitude to the English at this time was mild by comparison: in a period of near-anglomania in Germany Andreas Riem's vitriolic account of his travels through England (1798–9) show him to be a surprisingly isolated anglophobe. Wendeborn, on the other hand, whose avowed intention was to correct the romantic descriptions of England by anglomanes, seems to find few faults, and excuses for most of them. Arndt is more severe in 1805 but, as will be seen later, modified his views in 1815. But before Waterloo the Second Anglo-American War brought the expected American censure of England, the best-known, perhaps, being Thomas Jefferson's 'England a pirate spreading misery and ruin over the face of the ocean', and of the English, 'commerce and a corrupt government have rotted them to the core'.

The year 1815 found Britain at the height of her power and influence, triumphantly convinced of the strength inherent in her democratic institutions: 'great and free, The dread and envy of them all', in the words of *Rule, Britannia*. But success engenders censure, ascendancy in trade gives rise to irritable references to a huckstering spirit, and the British idea of freedom, which might in essence be unassailable, could be taken to mean freedom for Britain to enjoy her own advantages. Friedrich List, writing in 1841 on the *National System of Political Economy*, talks of the clever device, by anyone reaching the summit of greatness, of kicking away the ladders by which he has climbed up; Britain, who had raised her manufacturing power and navigation by means of protective duties and restrictions on navigation to a point at which no one else can

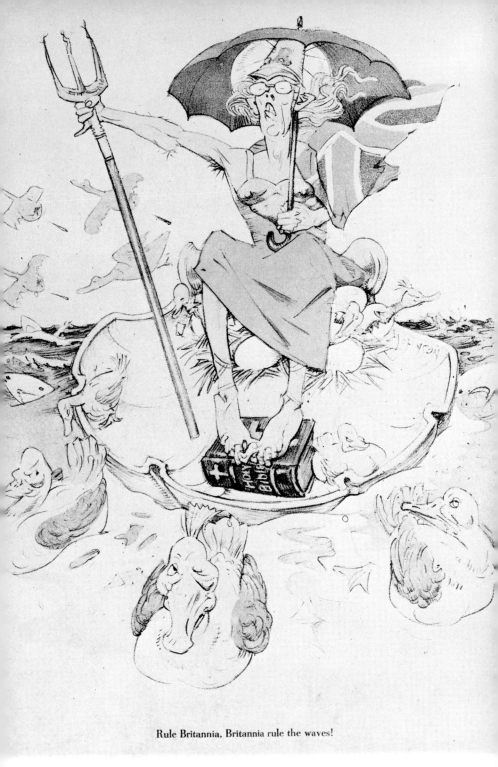

Rule Britannia, Britannia rule the waves!

3 'Hatching' Britain, *Kladderadatsch*, 1939

4 Cromwell as the Horrible Tail-Man,
Dutch cartoon, 1658, British Museum

compete, was now preaching free trade. The taunt of huckstering was frequent and will be discussed later. With regard to
freedom, Goethe, explaining to Eckermann in 1829 that the
British were unphilosophical, concluded that their motives
were always practical: they declaim against the inhuman
African slave trade, because they themselves had a use for the
blacks in West Africa, and had in any case founded large
colonies of negroes in America to supply the demand there.
While the Germans were philosophizing, the English 'laugh at
us and win the world'.

Nevertheless Palmerston was probably right when in 1832
he asserted that 'there never was a period when England was
more respected than at present in her foreign relations', and
thus, with the Euro-American defamatory chorus reduced to
pianissimo, Heine's vituperative strictures (e.g. 'the most
loathsome race that God ever created in his anger') struck a
louder note by contrast. Travellers and visitors came in hordes:
poets and artists (particularly French), German and Persian
princes, Italian counts, most of whom were either charmed
with England (or more often with Scotland) or published no
account of their reactions. Such criticisms as there were partly
reflect hackneyed foreign attitudes to a successful nation—
pride, arrogance, prejudice against everything non-English,
contempt for foreigners, shoving propensities, love of money
—and wishful thinking on the part of a few prophets of
England's downfall. The taunt that the people had an in-
ordinate love of titles apparently stemmed from the natural
curiosity of the islanders who would 'rush in crowds to stare at
a foreign prince', a curiosity that was probably misconstrued
as homage. All in all, always excepting Heine, and in spite of
the Anglo-French tension in 1840, there was really little serious
criticism until the middle of the century, at least in print.

It is doubtful, however, whether the period of seeming
quiescence gives a true picture of the American attitude to
England in the second quarter of the nineteenth century.
Anglophobia was apparently rife: memories of the Revolution
and of 1812, fostered by what Owen Wister (*A Straight Deal or
the Ancient Grudge*, 1920) calls 'astigmatic history teaching',
plus a certain resentment, probably exaggerated, of criticism of

America by well-known and well-loved British authors such as Dickens (*American Notes*, 1842 and *Martin Chuzzlewit*, 1843), could hardly be expected to produce more than a minority of American anglophiles. Comparatively few Americans had met other than immigrant Englishmen, in any case, and it is again significant that those who visited England were prepared to make more allowances than those who had not. Henry Adams's verdict was probably typical, 'Considering that I lose all patience with the English about fifteen times a day . . . I love them well'. But the bulk of Americans were convinced that England strongly resented the loss of the American colonies, and construed as chagrin what was merely indifference; and they still find it difficult to appreciate the point of the quip that Britain celebrates Thanksgiving Day on the fourth of July.

Until the mid-nineteenth century, German works on England had been mainly travel books, with notable exceptions such as Schopenhauer, Heeren, and List, whose comments on England were contained in works on philosophy or politics. The French observations were few. But in 1850 there appeared two objective accounts of England: Ledru-Rollin's *De la Décadence de l'Angleterre*, of which an English translation appeared almost simultaneously, and the last volume of Bignon's *Histoire de France*, which also prophesied England's downfall. As might be expected, however, the *rapprochement* between England and France during the Crimean War damped down the criticism for a time, although it was revived rapidly in the late '50s.

Other criticism was not entirely lacking. Emerson, who published his *English Traits* in 1856, after two visits to England, was, in spite of his friendship with poets such as Wordsworth and Coleridge, very frank about English shortcomings although, by the time of his death near the end of the century, many of his remarks could have applied equally well to his fellow Americans. In the '50s too, Karl Marx was already making forthright comments in his correspondence with Engels, and beginning to use British industrial development as the basis for a general assault on capitalism. But the bitterest American satire, being mostly unrecorded, made no impact except on English visitors to America. The anonymous author of *English Photographs* in 1869, describing the Independence Day celebrations, relates that 'at every gathering public speakers, more or less eloquent, bearded the British lion in his den, dragged him from his lair, trotted him up and down before the people, exposed his weaknesses as compared with the increasing might of the American eagle, and only refrained from turning the poor animal inside out, and tearing him to pieces, oratorically, upon condition that he would behave himself in future'. Apparently, however, as the lion could make no reply to the 'taunts and invective of the oratorical Wombwells and Van Amburghs', the spectators tired of the one-sided combat, and the lion of England disappeared from the Fourth of July celebrations, at least during the Civil War.

Nevertheless during this war feeling ran high against England, who began by showing sympathy with the South, and ended by inclining to the North, without, however, earning gratitude from the victors. After the war, a number of disputes, among which the *Alabama* case was the most prominent, embittered relations for several years, and carping comment ranged from the friendly remonstrances of Russell Lowell in the *Biglow Papers* to the bitter outbursts of the Fenians. But from the '70s to the middle '90s Anglo-American relations developed without noticeable tension, hence without noticeable additions to this anthology.

Relations between France and England took a somewhat curious course. In spite of their co-operation in the Crimean War, relations were strained at the end of the decade, and considerable ill-feeling lasted during the 1860s. Meanwhile Prussia was making her spectacular advances under Bismarck, much to the horror of the English liberals, whose criticisms were heartily resented in some German circles. Treitschke, who began by being a liberal, painted glowing pictures of England in the '50s, lost interest in the late '60s on the eve of German unity, and in his *History*, begun in the early '70s, sought to whip up Germany's national pride by bitter denunciation of England, contradicting many things he had said earlier. Of those closer to Bismarck, Lothar Bucher was probably England's chief critic, while Bismarck on occasion made a distinction between the reliability of the individual Englishman and the unreliability (and perfidy) of England. But on the whole England and Germany still regarded themselves as natural allies until the end of the century, after which the growing menace of the German navy finally forced England into the anti-German camp. Relations with France, although more or less amicable in the 1870s, deteriorated again as the result of the British occupation of Egypt in 1882, and it was not until the formation of the Entente Cordiale by the settlement of the Egyptian and Moroccan questions in 1904 that the modern era of Anglo-French friendship began.

The trends of the present century are too familiar to need elaboration. While there has been much foreign criticism, sometimes amply justified, sometimes silly, of individuals and customs, the main strictures have been on ideological rather than national lines, and the obloquy has been aimed not so much at England as such as at England as a typical example of bleating democracy, decadent liberalism, capitalist imperialism and the like. It is true, however, that at the lower levels of popular vituperation there was plentiful abuse on traditional lines. In both world wars England, although she was not Germany's sole opponent, seemed usually to be the main target for abuse. But in the 1914–18 war this was a verbal sniping from prominent individual Germans rather than a planned barrage from an anathematizing machine. In the second world war it is difficult to disentangle the genuine feeling of hostility of the German people from the propagandist outpourings of the hate campaign organized by Dr Goebbels; in any case the force of the invective was also directed against Jews and Russians, Poles and Czechs at the appropriate times, and Britain received the full blast only when she was the sole enemy in the second year of the war. But the blast was greater, not merely because of its concentration and planned strategy, but because the use of wireless helped to propel it to its target. Between the wars American isolationism produced the expected criticism of Britain, both from single writers like Ludwell Denny, G. H. Payne and Quincy Howe and from the Hearst-controlled press, as well as from such papers as the *Chicago Tribune*. Since the war conditions have greatly changed, although the immediate post-war period saw a curious outpouring of accumulated irritations and suspicions, partly no doubt a reaction from the enforced co-operativeness of the war years, partly due to ferocious support of the Zionist cause in the New York *P.M.* and other journals.

There have, then, been definite periods of anglophobia, giving rise to spates of hate literature, with little mitigating calm appraisal; the highlights being perhaps the Hundred Years War, the quarrel with Spain, the English Civil War and its repercussions, the Dutch Wars, the Anglo-American wars, the French Revolution, the Boer War and the two World Wars. But even in these periods not all England's enemies hated her, and it would be interesting (if impossible) to trace in every case whether the enmity was genuine, or touched off by some lone incident. In a few cases, particularly of the travellers, it is known what sparked off the fuse: seasickness in the Channel, affording a jaundiced view of England from the outset, bad weather, an uncomfortable inn, language misunderstandings and other chance happenings, none of which merited the general abuse of England which they occasioned. Riem, a great hater, came to England at the end of the eighteenth century, when anglomania in Germany was at its rifest, and after a stormy crossing had his books seized at the London custom-house and the leather bindings hacked off as contraband goods – small wonder that he declared this to be typical of the English character, the home 'of perjury and fraud'. De Saussure in 1725, Casanova in 1763, and Heine in 1827 were also incensed by the rudeness and brusqueness of the customs officials. A century earlier than Riem, however, Sorbière, who on the whole thought kindly of England, had found the customs civil, but at Dover children ran after him calling, 'A monsieur! A monsieur! French dog!' His journey in a stage-coach to London hardly put him in the right humour for appreciating the metropolis. Alexander Tille, a German lecturing in Glasgow University, was so incensed by the Boer War that he wrote scathingly of England in *Die Woche* and subsequently left Glasgow to return to Germany: the result was *Aus Englands Flegeljahren*.

But perhaps the most extreme example of momentarily invoked hate was the world-famous *Hassgesang* (Hymn of

Hate) of the first world war. Ernst Lissauer, sitting in a Hamburg café with journalist friends a few weeks after the war had begun, heard a report that England had held up an American hospital ship. Infuriated, he scribbled the song in the heat of the moment on a scrap of paper, apparently without the slightest intention of its going any further. But it was snatched up and published, sung by every German schoolgirl, and translated into every possible language. He made not a penny out of it, and later in life said that he was glad he had not, as he had never hated the English people. He afterwards turned pacifist, and died in America in 1937.

Other critics have modified their views or found it expedient to recant them. Pierre Loti was fiercely anti-English (*L'Inde sans les Anglais*, which he dedicated to President Kruger), but apparently mellowed considerably towards England after being received graciously by Queen Alexandra. The American evangelist, Dr Billy Graham, denounced England as a 'spiritual vacuum', but admitted in an interview with John Marshall of the *Daily Mail*, 'Those statements I made came out of ignorance and immaturity. I was wrong, utterly wrong.' Another American, Ambassador Mr Joseph P. Kennedy, had some harsh things to say about England in dispatches of 1940: twenty years later, in an interview with a *Daily Mail* reporter, he said, 'If I told you my thoughts about Britain now, you wouldn't be at all dismayed. In fact, I think everyone would be pretty pleased.' In 1947 the American playwright, Ben Hecht, published in the *New York Herald Tribune* a 'Letter to the Terrorists of Palestine' containing the famous lines, 'Every time you blow up a British arsenal, or wreck a British jail, or send a British railroad sky high, or rob a British bank, or let go with your guns and bombs at the British betrayers and invaders of your homeland, the Jews of America make a little holiday in their hearts', and this was included in his autobiography in 1954; but on a visit to England in 1955 he at first denied using the words. When confronted with them in print, he admitted he had written them 'at a time of high emotional feeling', and continued, 'I do not feel the same now. This is one of the finest countries in the world.' The late Professor G. J. Renier (*The English: Are they Human?*) is also reported as having had second thoughts about the English in a lecture he gave at the University of London, but if so, did not voice them in the second edition of his book, which appeared in 1947. The north German poet and patriot, Ernst Moritz Arndt, seemed to waver throughout his life between contempt and admiration for the English. He calls them 'half savages' (1805), naval despots (1806) and censures their 'petty shopkeeper politics' (1815). Yet in the same year he holds them up as a mirror to all Europe, and in the preface to the third edition of his *Geist der Zeit* (1815) apologizes to his compatriots (!) for his unjust verdict on the English, a judgement born of immaturity. Even Heine, after a forthright attack on 'Perfidious Albion' on 29 July 1840, admits on the 30th, 'Yesterday I said some very bitter things about the English. But it now appears that their guilt is not so great as I thought.'

And what are the accusations that have been hurled at England over all these centuries? First and foremost, perfidy: indeed, the title of this anthology might well have been 'Perfidious Albion'.[1] In the Middle Ages perfidy was not an exclusively English perquisite: countries freely applied it to each other, and a fifteenth-century author calls the Germans 'Teutonica gens perfida'. But as early as the late twelfth century Otto de Sancto Blasio had referred to 'Anglicam perfidiam', and it soon became a fixed notion in Europe that the English were un-reliable. In a *pièce farcie* of the thirteenth century there is an allusion to the 'faus Anglois', who gently say 'welcome', but are within 'pleni fraudibus'; in a fourteenth-century French manuscript a Latin couplet, which may be of earlier date, states that the Englishman is a crook who cannot be trusted, and that if he says 'hail' to you, beware of him as of an enemy. Proverbial sayings such as 'Loyaulté d'Angloys ne vault une poytevine' (which may be translated as 'English loyalty is not worth a brass farthing') remained current for centuries. Whether this denoted any real distrust of the English as such, or was just the sort of gibe that one applies to any enemy, is

---

[1] H. D. Schmidt, 'The idea and slogan of "Perfidious Albion"', *Journal of the History of Ideas* XIV, 4 (1953), pp. 604–16.

difficult to say. Few Frenchmen knew any Englishmen apart
from the soldiers on French soil, and the inhabitants of the
comparatively unknown island were dubbed 'tailed' anyway,
but the idea of disloyalty soon became associated with the
English treatment of their kings. Charles of Orleans, about the
year 1450, voices the general French feeling when he says,
'Have not the English often betrayed their kings?', a reference,
no doubt, to the violent deaths of Edward II and Richard II.
In the sixteenth century French verse makes frequent mention
of English 'infidelity' to their rulers, and the beheading of
Sir Thomas More and Anne Boleyn touches off more bitter
taunts of disloyalty: the Italian Scaliger, in his *Poeticas* (published posthumously in 1561) reviles the 'angli perfidi'
(followed by his eight other abusive adjectives), and with the
execution of Mary Queen of Scots, France's laments were laced
with loud cries of 'perfidy', usually coupled with accusations of
cruelty. 'Perfide et brutale', 'perfide Anglois, gent cruelle et
barbare', and of Elizabeth 'perfide, desloiale', make it clear
that the perfidy means faithlessness towards kings and queens.
In 1652 Bossuet interrupted one of his sermons in Metz to say
'L'Angleterre, ah! la perfide Angleterre!', and when James II
was exiled, Madame de Sévigné made her celebrated remark in
a letter, 'I think truly that the King and Queen of England are
better at St-Germain than in their perfidious kingdom'.

Thus far the 'perfidious' conduct had been domestic, but in
the eighteenth century in the eyes of the critics it became
diplomatic. Frederick the Great revived the 'perfidy' charge in
the sense of breaking faith with one's allies, and the French,
adopting this new meaning, made great play with it during the
Revolution, likening British loyalty to the Punic faith of
Carthage. In many French revolutionary poems England is
referred to as 'Albion', a term which goes back to classical
times but which now passed through irony to gibe, and it
seems inevitable, at least in retrospect, that 'perfidious' and
'Albion' should finally unite. The expression was used in 1809
and became more common during the later period of the
Empire. It finally came into its own with the Syrian crisis and
the rebirth of Bonapartism in 1840–1. Heine, who was in Paris
at the time, established the expression 'das perfide Albion' in

German, and from then on it seems to have been employed by any country having a disagreement with Britain. German historians used it, the German Emperor quoted it in 1901, Alfred Geiser adopted it as a title for his condemnatory work in 1915, and the Nazis made full use of it in the second world war. Like 'godons coués', it was too neat a catch-phrase to drop.

In the minds of the Continent, hypocrisy was frequently linked with perfidy, and even blamed as the cause. Geiser, mentioned above, speaks of Britain's 'persistent efforts to hide a selfish rapacity under a cloak of morality and idealism', a 'masterly hypocrisy, which has earned for England the name of "Perfidious Albion" '. Similarly, Bismarck attacked the 'perfidy and hypocrisy' of the British government, and almost every German diatribe alludes to them separately or together. Spiridion Gopčević, a Czech who published a philippic on England in 1915, attacks 'pharisaically pious Albion' and calls his work *The Land of Unlimited Hypocrisy*. It was a charge often made by Karl Marx, who asserted that the British hid their egotism under the 'vilest hypocrisy' and supported his statement by references to the treatment of the colonies, and the Nazis dug it up again for use as one of their stereotyped insults before and during the second world war. 'Hypocrisy, thy name is England' exclaimed the *Westdeutscher Beobachter* of 31 March 1939. But the German word *Heuchelei* was an unhandy word, compared with the English 'cant', which had graduated by the eighteenth century from its early meaning of 'whining incantation' to 'hypocritical utterances'; and so the German historians adopted the English word in the sense of 'religious or political moralizing', coupled, of course, with the insinuation that English speech was at variance with English actions. Thus it came to mean 'political insincerity', a natural concomitant of perfidy. It was Jefferson, however, who in 1810 referred to the Punic faith of England as the 'faith of a nation of merchants', and we may at this point consider the second slogan, almost as well-known as 'Perfidious Albion', that England is a 'nation of shopkeepers'.

It would be refreshing if we could here and now finally dispose of the statement, still repeated *ad nauseam*, that Napoleon invented the term. He was not only not the first to use the expression, but he denied that he had ever meant it. On 17 February 1817, in a conversation with Barry O'Meara on St Helena, Napoleon quoted Paoli as having said, 'They are a nation of merchants, and generally have a gain in view. Whenever they do anything, they always calculate what profit they shall have from it. They are the most calculating people in existence.' Napoleon then added, 'Now I believe Paoli was right.' A few months later (31 May) the Emperor alluded to O'Meara's resentment at the use of the term 'nation of shopkeepers'. 'No such thing was ever intended. I meant that you were a nation of merchants, and that all your great riches, and your grand resources arose from commerce, which is true.' Thus when the late Dean Inge, repeating the myth that Napoleon coined the expression, commented that it would have been more true to say that England had excelled in manufactures and commerce, he was suggesting that Napoleon should have said what in fact he declared he had meant. Bertrand Barère, however, had certainly called England 'une nation boutiquière' in 1794, and in a widely quoted speech. In spite of this, and Napoleon's denial, the remark 'nation of shopkeepers' was attributed to Napoleon, even in his own day. Prinz Pückler-Muskau, in his travel diary of 1826–9, says on 5 October 1826 that London 'has the air of a seat of government, and not of an immeasurable metropolis of "shopkeepers", to use Napoleon's expression'.

But the expression was, as so many other gibes current abroad, of English origin. Adam Smith, in Book IV of his *Wealth of Nations* (1776), declared that 'to found a great empire for the sole purpose of raising up a people of customers, may at first sight appear a project fit only for a nation of shopkeepers', and the phrase was used on 1 August of the same year by Samuel Adams, speaking in the State House, Philadelphia. But ten years earlier the Dean of Gloucester, Josiah Tucker, had stated in the third of his *Four Tracts*, 'A shopkeeper will never get the more custom by beating his customers, and what is true of a shopkeeper is true of a shopkeeping nation'. The term seems therefore to have been current in England in the eighteenth century (and accepted there as a bald statement of fact) and was then adopted as a mild form of abuse by foreigners. The Germans certainly branded England as a 'Krämervolk' in the nineteenth century, and Bismarck, in a conversation with von Tirpitz in 1897, said that the English had the souls of hucksters. The shopkeeper theme was much revived in the first world war: Werner Sombart talks of 'the great shop, England', and Pastors Rump, Tolzien, and Vorwerk refer to a 'nation of hucksters', 'shop-keeper spite', and 'a huckstering spirit'. In 1918, however, H. G. Wells, in *Joan and Peter*, made Oswald Sydenham say that 'we were becoming a boastful and a sprawling people. The idea of grabbing half the world — and then shutting other people out with tariffs, was . . . a "shoving tradesmen's dream".' Thus in the end even the English came to use it as a gibe.

Shopkeeping involves money; England was thus branded with a greed for lucre. Rousseau, in a note written in on the manuscript of his *Projet de Constitution pour la Corse* (1765), states baldly that the English public does not love liberty for its own sake, but because it produces money, and Riem in 1798 refers to 'those wealthy muck-worms who extorted millions in India and owe their fortunes to trade'. Caricatures show John Bull clutching money-bags, Max O'Rell (Paul Blouet) in 1883 pictures John Bull on his deathbed as saying, 'My son, get money, honestly if you can; but get money', and the theme was much laboured in the first world war. Helfferich, in December 1914, speaking in the Reichstag, declared that 'For England power and gold are inseparable conceptions. The British world empire is largely built up on British money power and will hold together with it.' Pastor Tolzien averred that England declared war from shopkeeper spite, wanting to 'earn the thirty pieces of silver', and the American Ludwell Denny, in 1930, that she was exacting tribute from the rest of the world. 'She [Britain] grew rich. She put her profits back into world investments, and into a navy to perpetuate her holdings and her power. Whenever a serious competitor arose, she eliminated that competitor by war. Germany was not the first — and may not be the last.' From the late eighteenth century to the present day Britain's critics and enviers have rung the changes on the theme of robber politics.

The charge of piracy on the high seas goes back much

further. Sidonius Apollinaris wrote of the Saxon pirate in the fifth century. Hentzner, who came to England during the reign of Elizabeth I, called the English 'good sailors, and better pirates, cunning, treacherous and thievish'. All the countries who have had to meet the British navy have at one time or another used what is, after all, the most obvious insult to hurl at sailors of a predominant naval power, systematically using the weapon of economic blockade. The *Ode aux Français* of 1804 calls the British 'pirates', 'naval despots', 'haughty vandals', 'vampires', 'tyrants', 'Neros', as well as accusing them of perfidy and other Punic qualities, and in 1810 Jefferson denounced England as a 'pirate spreading ruin and misery over the face of the ocean'. The sea blockade of the first world war revived the taunt, with paraphrases such as 'vile and grossly abused mastery of the seas', 'mercantile policy of violence', 'barbarism in international law'; in 1919 Spengler discusses 'the pirate instinct of the island people' and talks of their 'plundering world economy'. It is a moot point how far the gibe owes its survival to the fact that pirates are colourful characters like *godons coués*.

The other main indictment levelled at Britain as a nation was on the score of imperialism. The word 'imperialism', which had never been applied to the British Empire before 1868, began to be so applied in an increasingly derogatory sense after 1876. The relationship between colonies and mother country could never remain static for long, and the collapse of the four great colonial empires—the French, British, Spanish, and Portuguese—between 1763 and 1824 had encouraged a widespread scepticism as to the value of colonies in any form. They were expensive to maintain and defend, and ungrateful; they would drop off the parent tree like ripe fruit when mature enough. In spite, however, of this anti-colonial sentiment, which dominated English political thinking for fifty years and was reinforced in its economic aspects by the passionate belief in free trade, the Empire did not collapse. It was expanding again, primarily for strategical reasons, in the late nineteenth century, although responsible opinion in every political party was coming to accept complete self-government as the ultimate destiny of the Commonwealth. The radical conscience could not explain this expansion except in terms of political domination and economic exploitation. Americans in particular found it hard to believe that the great self-governing Dominions had a genuine sentimental attachment to the 'old country'. It was an English radical, J. A. Hobson, who in 1902 popularized the theory that the essential force behind British colonial activity was neither paternalism nor emigration nor even trade but the search by 'economic parasites' for bigger investments than were available in the home market. In spite of repeated proofs during the next half-century that British capital investment usually preferred other outlets, the theory was seized on by Lenin, and Britain remained in Communist eyes the supreme example of imperialism as the last stage of decadent capitalism. The term gradually became so universally convenient, however, for purposes of international invective that the 'imperialist' is now the twentieth-century version of the devil, and the word has ceased to have a predominantly British application.[1]

A few of the critics make it clear that their target is not the individual Englishman, but the nation, its politics, its government. Thus Bismarck finds the Englishman decent, estimable and trustworthy ('lying is to him the most serious reproach one can make') but English politics show 'incredible limits of hypocrisy and perfidy', and Goncourt calls the English sharpers as a nation but honest as individuals. Saul K. Padover, writing in the American paper *P.M.* in August 1946, asserts that they have changed little in 136 years. He recalls that in 1810 Thomas Jefferson remarked, 'The British government present the singular phenomenon of a nation, the individuals of which are as faithful to their private engagements and duties, as honorable, as worthy, as those of any nation on earth, and whose government is yet the most unprincipled at this day known.' There are probably few governments of which this

[1] All these points are fully discussed and illustrated as a problem in semantics by R. Koebner and H. D. Schmidt, *Imperialism, The Story and Significance of a Political Word, 1840–1960* (1964), pp. xxiii, 28–9, 176, and chaps. 6, 7, 8, 11, and 12 generally.

has not been said at some time or another by their more energetic critics. England has said it of other countries, and in the guise of a Spaniard, Espriella, an Englishman (Robert Southey) said it of England. But not all the critics have been content to limit themselves to these left-handed compliments, and an attempt will now be made to review briefly the multifarious criticisms that have been uttered about the English people, as distinct from the English government, and to put them as far as possible into perspective.

As will be seen from the classification of the extracts in this anthology, censure ranges over the fields of English social and domestic life, the arts, religion, the intellect, character and appearance of the English, and from high-minded animadversions on English racial intolerance to snide comments on English false teeth. By far the greatest number of quotations relate to character. When Virgil, in 37 B.C., talked of the Britons 'sundered from all the world', he may or may not have been referring to their mental attitude, but certainly Horace, in 23 B.C., said that they were 'no friends to strangers'. In 1962 an American professor called them 'God's frozen people' and in the intervening two millennia numerous visitors have recorded the unwelcoming attitude of the English. 'Antipathy for foreigners' (Trevisano, 1500), 'despising foreigners' (Meteren, 1599), 'England isolated like the lone vulture in its eyrie' (Ledru-Rollin, 1850), 'attitude of insular superiority and contempt for everything foreign' (G. B. Adams, 1896) are samples; Hansen said that the English inhabit not merely an island of their own but a cosmic plane which foreigners cannot penetrate, and Emerson's oft-quoted remark that 'every one of these islanders is an island himself' had been anticipated by Novalis, Montesquieu, and others. The islanders were found to be silent, immersed in their newspapers in the taverns, morose, 'moving about heavily and in silence', refusing to speak unless introduced. Heine wrote, 'Silence—a conversation with an Englishman'. (Erasmus would not have agreed: he was delighted with the friendliness of the early Tudors and the frequent kissing and greeting.) And coupled with this aloofness towards other nations was the alleged besetting failing, national pride and arrogance.

In the late fourteenth century Froissart, to quote Lord Berners' translation of 1525, declared that the 'Englysshe men were so prowde that they set nothyng by ony nacyon but by theyr owne', and in 1429 the unknown poet of the *Ballade contre les Anglais* said that they had long behaved in too proud a manner ('De tropt orgouilleuse manière Longuemen vous estes tenus'). Since then the charge has cropped up with monotonous regularity, sometimes in the form of the well-worn statement that whenever they see a likeable foreigner they say, 'What a pity he is not an Englishman!' or 'he looks like an Englishman' (cf. *Venetian Relation, c.* 1500). Other paraphrases were 'intoxicated with the idea of their own importance' (Duc de Sully, 1603), 'cold, proud, haughty and vain' (Diderot, 1765), 'only the Englishman is the *ne plus ultra* of perfection, and Nature's masterpiece' (Riem, 1798), 'the haughtiest flag that floats' (J. J. Roche, 1895), 'insolent and overbearing' (Emperor Wilhelm II of Germany, 1904). Thus for six centuries they have been looked upon as proud, arrogant, egoistical, aloof, insular, and unfriendly to other nationalities, in spite of having kept almost open house, both in peace and war, for refugees of every description and denomination (who at times have shown a curious nostalgia for the brutal disciplines from which they have fled). In lumping together pride, arrogance, egoism, and aloofness certain of the critics have shown less than perspicacity. Pride may have been a monastic sin: pride in one's country which, after all, is equally felt by Americans, Frenchmen, Germans, Spaniards and the rest, is more usually a symbol of national virtue. So it is better not to make too much of British 'pride' at a time when so many newly independent nations are showing immense satisfaction with their youthful achievements. The American, Owen Wister, defends English pride ('England has, after all, a thousand years of greatness to her credit. Who would not be proud of that?') but censures arrogance, 'the seamy side of pride'. Nor is egoism necessarily an unmixed national sin, nor an English monopoly: von Bülow said in 1914, alluding to the phrase 'perfide Albion', 'In reality, this supposed treachery is nothing but a sound and justifiable egoism, which together with other great qualities of the English people, other nations would do well to imitate' (he left it out of the revised edition, however, in 1916). It is doubtful whether even all English people would go so far in the defence of perfidy, but might prefer the more cautious statement of Havelock Ellis, that 'the pronounced individuality of a highly selected people has inevitably led to the exhibition of great qualities balanced by the great defects of those qualities'. Thus egoism has its obverse and reverse and may just as easily argue a strong individualism as a blameworthy arrogance. But the coupling of aloofness with pride is, while eminently understandable, perhaps widest of the mark.

The English stiff upper lip has always been an enigma to the non-English. The exhibitors of it have been variously described as 'wooden', 'machine-like', 'automatons', 'insensible', 'unfeeling', but at least Taine (1863) calls it 'acquired insensibility' and recognizes it for what it is—a product of British education. It is one of the things the English admit, while disagreeing as to its interpretation. Is it One-Upmanship, or what Mr Edmund Wilson regarded in 1948 as a tactical form of 'British rudeness'? He called it a 'form of good manners', 'a game to put your opponent at a disadvantage', where 'good breeding is something you exhibit by snubbing and scoring off people'. M. Pierre Daninos put it in another way when he said (1955), 'One of the most striking superiorities of the English is the way they manage to give a foreigner an inferiority complex the moment he sets foot in the country'. It may be that Senator Wheeler, of Montana, meant the same thing when he denied in 1943 that the Americans dislike the English. 'I like England, and I like the English people, but the fact is that you are too damned smart for us poor simple-minded saps over here.' And Mr Drew Middleton, who complains of so little in England, remarks, 'When an Englishman, especially an upper-class Englishman, desires to be rude, he makes the late Mr Vishinsky sound like a curate.'

The strong individualism in the Englishman, produced, according to Havelock Ellis 'by a process of marine selection', has contributed as much to the reputation for insularity as has the fact that he actually inhabits an island which has not been conquered for a thousand years. But the foreigner notes a singular paradox: this individualism, inherited in part from the piratical adventurousness which brought the successive invaders to the island, is combined in the English nature with a respect for law and order and formality. Many foreign critics have commented on the contrasts in the English character (Prinz Pückler-Muskau, already mentioned, was one, and his account much interested Goethe), but it is doubtful whether they have really understood how the paradox evolved, or how it works. In fact, it is a mystery to most of the English. But the net result is that they are looked upon by their kindlier commentators as eccentric (thus Santayana, 'England is the paradise of individuality, eccentricity, heresy, anomalies, hobbies and humours') and by their sterner critics as mad, a notion that they themselves favour at times. First mentioned by the French in 1429 in the *Ballade contre les Anglais* ('in France you are treated as madmen'), the subject of English madness still continues to fascinate foreigners: in 1952 Señor Madariaga wrote that it 'seems plain to the average Spaniard that one cannot be English without being somewhat queer and even downright mad', and offered the explanation that 'the English enjoy madness as a liberation from their usual objectivity'. Stendhal (*Le Rouge et le Noir*, 1831) makes Julien say that the 'wisest Englishman is mad for an hour every day', which is probably more than the average Englishman has time for, but a great number of them do find time for it on at least three occasions: royal ceremonies, football matches, and bank holidays. No doubt too the habit of referring to a dear friend with the words, 'Oh, he's quite mad' (or 'crazy'), is taken too literally by some Continentals.

Brutality has always ranked as a major British sin. In the seventh century Bishop Isidore of Seville said that the British were so named because of their brutish character ('Britones, nominatos quidam suspiciantur eo quod bruti sunt') and in the late Middle Ages it was doubtless English soldiers fighting on foreign soil who kept up this reputation. Van Meteren, in his history of the Netherlands (1599) certainly spoke of English cruelty in war, and Coulon, in 1654, asserted that the island, once the abode of angels and saints, was now the 'hell of demons and parricides'. This statement was doubtless

D

prompted by the execution of Charles I: as has been shown
earlier, the many royal beheadings had profoundly shocked the
Continent and incurred the frequent charges of perfidy, and in
the seventeenth century cruelty, with which the English had
also been sporadically charged in French literature of the Tudor
period, now appeared in almost every political diatribe.
'Accursed, cruel and mad' ('maudits, cruels et forcenés') runs
through the poems almost like a refrain. Travellers, as has
been noted, quote the love of cruel sports and public executions, and the nation's delight in a drama 'full of bleeding
corpses' (St Evremond, 1662), while in more recent times
Nietzsche called the English more brutal than the Germans.
The first world war brought more accusations of English
barbarity, and E. Schultze declared in 1940 (*Die Blutspur
Englands*), presumably to reassure his German readers, that no
nation had committed a greater number of atrocities than
England. Foreigners also condemn the pursuit of blood sports
(although other countries still hunt!) and this is probably an
echo of vehement criticism by the English themselves.
Similarly, occasional foreign allusions to the ill-treatment of
children in England seem to be based on the wide publicity
given to certain cases by the British press, just as the alien
outcry over examples of nineteenth-century cruelty was to a
large extent prompted by the exposures of Dickens and other
writers. Rousseau (in *Émile*) ascribed the brutality and blood-
thirstiness of Englishmen to the fact that they were great
meat-eaters, although he was not the first to suggest it, but
G. Le Sage (1715) thought that the addiction to violent sports
was rather a manifestation of coarseness. Wendeborn finds in
it a relic of the Roman occupation.

As cruelty is sometimes, although not always, a result of
passion, anger is another sin often chalked up against the
English. In the fourteenth century Froissart said that they were
'the peryloust people of the worlde, and most outragyoust if
they be up' (Lord Berners' rendering) and the many French
vituperative poems of the sixteenth and seventeenth centuries
refer constantly to 'ces enragés'. They are bad-tempered,
surly, and morose: the Swiss Muralt, in his *Lettres sur les
Anglois* (1725, published in English in 1726) found the English

'furious in anger, to a Degree of beating their Faces with their Fists . . . on trifling occasions', and Heine, in his *Englische Fragmente* (1828) begged that no poet or dreamer should ever be sent to London—he would simply get shoved or knocked down by an Englishman in a hurry saying 'God Damn!'. Notoriety as 'mighty swearers' undoubtedly enhanced the British reputation for anger and bad temper: as already mentioned, 'godons' (goddams) had become the recognized synonym for 'English', often in the combination 'godons coués', as early as the late fourteenth century. The word 'godon' began to lose its connection with foul language in the sixteenth century and will be further discussed under 'gluttony', but this did not mean that the islanders ceased to swear. On the whole it was English soldiers on the Continent who sprinkled their language with oaths, although de Saussure in 1725 found the English naval officers at Portsmouth 'the most terrible swearers' he had ever come across ('Good Lord! What men!' he exclaims), and Beaumarchais, in the third act of the *Barber of Seville* (1775) refers to English as 'a fine language: it is founded on "God Damn" '. It is doubtful whether swearing would be thought an especial prerogative of Englishmen today, and indeed it is hard to believe that in the early nineteenth century the London businessmen in Cheapside rushed about pushing people aside with oaths. Oddly enough, however, the English themselves do admit to anger: in 1951 Mr Geoffrey Gorer, in order to gather material for his *Exploring English Character* (1955), devised a questionnaire on all aspects of English life, which was sent to thousands of readers of *The People*, and subsequently studied by the Research Section of Odhams Press Ltd. Of his sample of 5,000 answers, 50 per cent admitted to anger, if by 'anger' was meant nagging, bad temper, and surliness, but 66 per cent if domineering and obstinacy are included. It may be that there is still a great deal of latent anger in the English (apart from the peevish adolescents, somewhat too flatteringly described at one time as the Angry Young men) and that English education and public opinion keep it in check, until a righteous cause allows them to unleash their indignation with a clear conscience.

The surliness that goes with bad temper was often close to

melancholy, and the English word 'spleen' could mean either; but the 'spleen' that was so very English was a deep melancholy which could lead to suicide. Casanova relates in his memoirs that after his mistress Pauline had deserted him in 1763 he was overcome by 'un véritable spleen britannique', and three decades earlier the Englishman George Cheyne had published a work on *The English Malady*. He says that the title was a reproach universally thrown on the island by foreigners, 'by whom nervous Distempers, Spleen, Vapours, Lowness of Spirits, are in Derision, called the English Malady'. He suggested as the cause of this peculiarly English depression the moisture of the air, the richness and heaviness of the food, 'the Inactivity and sedentary Occupations of the better Sort (among whom this evil mostly rages)' and the unhealthy town life, which 'have brought forth a Class and Set of Distempers, with atrocious and frightful Symptoms, scarce known to our Ancestors'. Le Sage, in 1715, had commented on it and explained that some attribute it 'to the heaviness of the sea air and others to the coarseness of the food, particularly too much meat-eating', and about the same time Destouches wrote the mock epitaph, 'Here lies John Roast-Beef, Esquire, Who hanged himself, to pass the time' ('ci-gît Jean Rosbif, escuyer, Qui se pendit pour se désennuyer'). Voltaire, recounting an English suicide in 1733, wrested from the silent, brooding Englishmen in an inn the statement that it had happened because 'the wind was in the east'. The east wind is often blamed (apparently by the English) for the tendency to gloom, taciturnity and suicide, although the anonymous French author of *The English Nation, puffed up with Pride, Beer and Tea* (1803) quotes autumn as the suicide season, when the east wind does not prevail. Napoleon blamed the climate; Wendeborn, who at least had observed the English for twenty-two years, gave it as his opinion in 1791 that climate and meat-eating were not the cause, but education, which was much too free. In none of these accounts is there any suggestion of a serious reason for the English suicides: Goethe, in his *Dichtung und Wahrheit*, says, 'It is related of an Englishman that he hanged himself, to avoid the daily task of dressing and undressing'. In the absence of reliable statistics for the eighteenth century, it is impossible to say whether there were in fact proportionately more suicides in England than in other countries: but at least Edward Young's exclamation in his *Night Thoughts* (1742–4), 'O Britain, infamous for suicide', confirms Britain's reputation in this respect. Donne's *Biathanatos* (published 1648) and Hume's *Of Suicide, or Self-murder* (1742) had publicized the supposed peculiarly English habit. It is clear, however, from late nineteenth-century surveys that by then Great Britain's percentage was less than a quarter of the high rate obtaining in some other European countries. Recent statistics available for the 1950s show nine European countries with higher rates than in England.

Whether or not excessive meat-eating was the cause of the English Malady (or its antidote), it is a fact that the English were considered great gluttons. The late fourteenth-century *Dispute between an Englishman and a Frenchman*, already alluded to, contains the statement, 'Their stomach is their god, and to the stomach they eagerly pay sacrifice' (*venter eorum est deus, et ventri sacrificare student*), and the Venetians, a century later, said that even when the war was raging most furiously, 'they will seek for good eating . . . without thinking of what harm might befal them'. The Greek Nicander Nucius, in 1545, called them 'Flesh-eaters and insatiable of animal food; sottish and unrestrained in their appetites', and the various proverbs current in the late Middle Ages for 'drunk (or gorged) like an Englishman' show the idea to be firmly established. Rabelais and others quote 'Anglia potat' and 'Englés borracho'. In the sixteenth century the word 'godons', which originally meant 'goddams', began to acquire the meaning of 'those who make gods of their stomachs', and Cotgrave, in his *French–English Dictionary* of 1650, translates 'godons' as 'a filthie glutton or swiller; one that hath a vile, wide swallow'. Sorbière said in 1663 that 'the English may be easily brought to anything, provided you fill their Bellies', and associates it with their great laziness, which will be commented on later. Others, such as the visitors Muralt and Misson de Valbourg, refer to English self-indulgence in the same century, and in the eighteenth the subject is aired by many, including de Saussure, Rousseau and Riem. The last-named castigates the 'gorging, swilling and whoring' (1798), and in the early nineteenth century the *Notes sur l'Angleterre* of Montesquieu[1] and the *Letters* of the Englishman Robert Southey (disguised as the Spaniard Espriella) mention the 'prodigious meat-eating'. Taine, in his *Notes sur l'Angleterre* (1871) was particularly unchivalrous: discussing the appearance of the English, he refers to ladies' faces which 'have become ruddy, and turned to raw beefsteak' and to the 'large front of white teeth, the projecting jaws of carnivora'. This is only surpassed by his revolting picture of the English male: overfed, fleshy ('in presence of this mass of flesh one thought of a beast for the butcher, and quietly computed twenty stones of meat'), and towards fifty, 'owing to the effect of the same diet seasoned with port wine, the figure and the face are spoiled, the teeth protrude . . . the brute brutalized'. He then describes the leaner type: 'Lessen the quantity of blood and fat . . . after the portly animal, after the overfed animal, comes the fierce animal, the English bull.' After this the remarks of the Indian Malabari in 1893 on the 'phenomenal bibulousness of the Briton' seem quite mild: 'the drunkenness that debases, brutalizes, and maddens, seems to be peculiar to the British soil'. To the underfed, abstemious Englishman of the twentieth century this makes strange reading, and even more so after the self-denial and rationing of two world wars. In the self-evaluations requested by Mr Gorer in 1951 for his survey of English Character, hardly any admitted to the sin of gluttony, although a few to drunkenness. Yet the portly John Bull still remains the symbol of England, both in alien and in English caricature, and the foreigner, who complained earlier of the surfeit of food, now complains of the cooking.

In 1531 the Venetian, Savorgnano, found the English more discreet in drinking than the Germans, but more idle. In the next century de Sorbière was quite eloquent on the subject of English inertia, declaring that these people were naturally lazy, and spent half their time taking tobacco, 'for they do perhaps glory in their Sloth, and believe that true Living consists in their knowing how to live at Ease'. Even the English labourers, according to La Rochefoucauld (1784), worked in a very casual manner and took frequent rests. There was less

[1] Published posthumously: Montesquieu died in 1755.

talk in the nineteenth century of laziness, but frequent allusions to sluggish or phlegmatic temperament (Emerson, Taine, and Steffen). In this present century Englishmen are either no longer considered lazy, or foreign critics have too much else to vilify to mention it. One finds occasional references, as for instance in Mrs Halsey's *With Malice toward Some* (1938), which contains all the clichés, well-worn and outworn, but on the whole it is not one of the present English vices.

Greed, covetousness, envy of other nations, a thirst for gain, coupled with a huckstering spirit, have also been labelled British, so much so that Pastor Vorwerk, in 1915, says that the Germans have now cast these sins from them, 'just because it is all British'. It was, of course, inevitable that after vast acquisitions of foreign trade and colonial territory they should be considered 'grasping', and also envious. According to Mr Gorer, the English themselves do not admit to envy: either they do not consider it a sin (Mr Gorer thinks it may be the English blind spot) or perhaps they realize that envy is too universal a characteristic of men and nations to be specifically English at all.

These are, however, only a few of the indictments of the English. There is also licentiousness: Muralt lists their amusements as 'Wine, Women and Dice, or, in a word, Debauchery' (1726); de Saussure says that 'Debauch runs riot with an un-blushing countenance' (1725), and Riem, as already mentioned, accuses them of whoring, together with gorging and swilling (1798). However, this gibe more or less died down during the nineteenth century, to be succeeded by criticisms of prudery, inhibitions, and even a frigid lack of interest in sex altogether. Only in the 1960s, when Britain has never had it so good, is teenage promiscuity beginning to restore belief in the country's romantic possibilities.

Now what must surely strike the reader as he looks back over this catalogue of foreign grievances is their very general character. They could be applied to most peoples of the world and at most stages of history. What people, after all, could not have been accused, at some time or another of pride, anger, sloth, lust, greed, gluttony and envy? They are no more than the seven deadly sins, which the medieval church well knew to be of universal application. For good measure, perfidy is thrown into the English list as an eighth, but again it would be difficult to maintain that the English are more vulnerable to accusations of perfidy in its present sense than other nations. Perhaps when we come to the more personal allusions, such as appearance, or the dullness of the English Sunday (though this, too, has Protestant affinities abroad), we come nearer to some exclusively English characteristics.

Remarks on appearance are, in fact, sparse, and in the main relate to the John Bull figure, which has largely disappeared now from the English scene. In *The England of Today* (1892) the Portuguese Oliveira Martins has described the more agile type that had evolved from the former John Bull, although his unflattering description could by no means have applied to all inhabitants. It may be true that Englishwomen have larger feet than many continentals (although America gives this distinction to the Swedes), and that some may have longer faces and redder complexions than the pale faces of the continent. Remarks about dentures, and criticisms of English shoe manufacture (both M. Halsey, 1938) are of doubtful application: many American women covet English-made shoes, and even buy them.

The English are hopeless in all the arts: 'unsculptural' (Pevsner, Reith Lectures, 1955), 'in exquisite arts not so well furnished' (Levinus Lemnius, 1561), 'not fertile soil for the fine arts' (Voltaire, 1744), 'of the arts they have no more notion than my cat' (Merimée, 1874), 'there is nothing on earth more terrible than English music, except English painting' (Heine, 1840), 'English painting is entirely derivative' (Renier, 1931), 'no ear either for rhythm or dancing' (Heine, 1840), 'as awkward at a frolic as a bear at a dance' (Horace Greeley, 1851), 'he has neither rhythm nor dance in the movements of his soul and body' (Nietzsche, 1886), 'their architecture is the laughing-stock of the Western world' (Renier, 1931), to quote but a few of the oft-repeated clichés. Even the drama is under fire: Goethe castigated its form, action and content (this was in his classical period), and Tolstoi called

Shakespeare 'an insignificant, inartistic writer', and declared that he 'cannot be recognized either as a great genius, or even as an average writer' (1904). Their manner of walking 'straight before them like mad dogs' (Emerson, 1856, quoting the French), 'like odious automatons, machines propelled by egoism' (Heine, 1842), of speaking, 'their elocution is stomachic' (Emerson, 1856), 'hesitating, humming and drawling are the three graces of the English conversation' (Boutmy, 1901, quoting another wit), and their behaviour generally, 'the English are not made of polishable substance' (Nathaniel Hawthorne, 1854), 'the English people are naturally ill-mannered and uncouth' (Boutmy, 1901), are all attacked. Then, too, they are considered to be bad linguists, bad philosophers, unable to generalize or deal with abstractions, uninventive, uncritical, intellectually arid. The list is far from complete. English religion, its form, its sincerity and its effects are much criticized, together with the clergy; and English pride and greed are carried over into this sphere too. According to Max O'Rell (Paul Blouet) John Bull 'knocked down to himself the Kingdom of Heaven—in his eyes as incontestably a British possession as India or Australia'.

The social system is attacked as artificial, especially so by Emerson. 'Their social classes are made by statute', 'their system of education is factitious', 'the manners and customs of society are artificial; made-up men with made-up manners; and thus the whole is Birminghamized, and we have a nation whose existence is a work of art.' Napoleon had much to say about the English ruling classes, and forecast in 1821 that one day John Bull would turn against them and hang the lot. He said that the aristocratic families made all the laws, which 'only exist to keep the rabble in order', and Emerson called English law 'a network of fictions'. In an interview with the *Daily Mail* in 1960 Mrs Pandit declared, 'You are still terrible snobs, with a caste system far more rigid than our own.' The houses are censured, either because the windows let in too much air, or not enough, or because, built in the nineteenth century or earlier, they do not conform to the most up-to-date American pattern of the mid-twentieth century. Americans in particular seem surprised that the hotels in England's ancient cathedral towns are not steel and concrete edifices with chromium fittings and the last word in plumbing and air conditioning.

No foreign book on England in this century would be complete without the stock banalities about English cooking. They are now so stereotyped that they almost give the impression that the foreigner has written up those paragraphs before disembarking at Dover or Southampton. But it was not always so. In the late fifteenth century the Venetians spoke of the 'excellent victuals' (1497), and Van Meteren (1575) found that the English ate 'well and delicately'; the German Platter, in 1599, was lyrical about their banquets. In the seventeenth century the Frenchmen Sorbière and Misson de Valbourg liked less the great quantities of meat, but the latter, unless he had his tongue in his cheek as he tasted the puddings, was quite ecstatic in his praise of them. In the nineteenth century the Austrian Grillparzer gives mouth-watering accounts of the turtle soup, excellent fish, and sirloin of beef he was served in a Strand chop-house, and in 1855 the American Nathaniel Hawthorne lists the delicacies he enjoyed at a civic banquet. (It is interesting to hear that he also thought the English better housed than the Americans, finding the houses 'a great deal newer than in our new country'.) In fact, the excellence of English food and cooking was such a byword that the complaints of earlier days must have come mostly from stomachs queasy after the Channel crossing. Even the nineteenth century produced few disparaging remarks, except for the familiar lament for the lack of sauces ('England has sixty religious sects, but only one sauce', attributed to Caraccioli amongst others, but to many others after him). There may be some psychological reason why the English prefer their good meat undisguised, or it may be a sign of the laziness which foreigners impute to them. But it was not until the 1930s that gibes about the cooking became an essential part of any foreign book on England, to be repeated *ad nauseam* in the '40s, with a complete disregard of the lingering rationing restrictions. Most fair-minded Englishmen will concede that the cooking in the lower-priced restaurants does not (and cannot) present the best of English fare, and yet Americans, having warned the would-be traveller to the United States that he cannot get a passable meal there under five dollars, will complain sarcastically of the ninety-five cent three-course lunch they have just consumed in an English café. This constant carping comes oddly from a country where 'French' fried potatoes and 'Spanish' rice are decanted from tins and warmed up. England has, however, even in this century, had its moments of triumph: in 1956 twelve nations competed in the Frankfurt International Cookery Competition, and when the English chefs arrayed their raw ingredients a French entrant sarcastically asked 'whether they were going to *cook* it'. The dogged English proceeded to do just that, and gave a public performance of the cooking *à l'anglaise* of 200 steak and kidney puddings, 250 roast Aylesbury ducklings and 150 roast grouse, which were consumed to the last morsel by the judges, and voted 'sensationnelle'. Nevertheless, the badness of English cooking has remained a cliché, although recently comments have begun to be more favourable.

The word 'English' itself is sometimes used with a slightly derogatory connotation. In the medieval *Roman de Renart* the fox trips his opponent by an English trick ('tor d'Englois') and a certain wrestling throw was known as a 'tor englois'. In the sixteenth century 'anglois' meant a creditor, and today 'être poursuivi par des Anglais' means to be pestered by creditors. 'Aller (or filer) à l'Anglaise' (in German 'sich englisch empfehlen') means to leave without permission, but here at least the English turn the tables on their accusers and call it 'taking French leave'. The American expression 'giving it English' means putting side (or a twist) on a ball; Mark Twain in 1870 spoke of 'putting the English' on a billiard ball, and 'giving it English' is still heard in American bowling alleys. It is doubtful, however, whether the French 'anglaiser' (German 'anglisieren') for the docking of a horse's tail was, or is, meant to be in any way disparaging.

From the foregoing discussion it is clear that there are few human defects not included in the comprehensive catalogue of English sins, although very few of the denigrators would hold all the English guilty of all of them all of the time. Foreign attempts to explain English oddities in speech and behaviour have produced some even odder results. Thus the expression 'I am afraid', prefixing a negative statement or refusal, has puzzled many. The Dane, Christen Hansen (*The English Smile*, 1935), asserts that when an Englishman says, 'I am afraid', he always means that he is damned sure; Tony Mayer (*La Vie Anglaise*, 1960) translates it as 'Et moi j'te dis que . . .', and in 1955 M. Pierre Daninos (*Major Thompson lives in France*) says that a woman who has just seen her husband set off for his office will, on answering the telephone, say, 'I am afraid he's out'. He does not perform the mental gymnastics of the late Professor Renier, who explains at length that if a person is asked at his own gate by a stranger if he may use his telephone, his supreme honesty will not allow him to state bluntly that he has no telephone, as it could, after all, have been installed since he left the house(!) It does not occur to any of these commentators that the Englishman is far from being so abrupt and impolite as he is painted, and that 'I am afraid' is simply a gentler and more circumlocutory form of refusal – the equivalent, in short, of 'I regret to say'.

The American Mrs Halsey, who has included in her *With Malice toward Some* (1938) most of the standard abuse of her hosts, concedes in her summing up, 'English life is seven-eighths below the surface, like an iceberg, and living in England for a year constitutes merely an introduction to an introduction to an introduction to it.' This does not, of course, prevent foreign visitors from writing authoritatively about England after a few weeks or months. Thus the most friendly accounts were often by foreigners whose stay was lengthy. Wendeborn had spent nearly fifteen years as pastor of the German church on Ludgate Hill before he published, in four volumes (1785–8), an impartial account of all aspects of English life, later translated by himself as *A View of England towards the Close of the Eighteenth Century*. Though far from uncritical, he considers that most writers on England have not stayed long enough to judge correctly. The Swedish Professor of History, Erik G. Geijer, who spent a year in England to learn the language, admits at the end of his *Impressions of England, 1809–1810*, that he came with prejudices against the people. He thought that British 'thirst for gain' and a 'narrow egotism' had stifled everything beautiful and noble, but concludes that the Swedish conception of egotism derives from an immature State, and that there is no more 'honest' person than the 'egotistic, industrious' Englishman. He praises the 'republican simplicity of manners' which is combined with a refinement 'perfect of its kind', the strictness of domestic manners compared with the ungoverned freedom of public life, the lack of luxury in the richest country in the world, the total absence of charlatanry, and earnestness even in malice ('a malice with a pistol in his hand'). He even finds honesty in the openness of English prostitution. After then declaring that one might go from one end of the earth to the other without finding anywhere 'the unpretending good sense, the respect for the law, the participation in and insight into the interests of the country which are so generally dispersed over this favoured island', Geijer refutes in advance any possible charges of Anglomania, says that he does not love England and would not like to live there. One staunch defender was the American, Owen Wister (*A Straight Deal, or the Ancient Grudge*, 1920). He condemns his countrymen for harbouring the ancient grudge, when England has far more reason to harbour grudges against France, and blames astigmatic history teaching in America with its anti-English, pro-French bias. He rejects the slur of 'Rude Britannia', arguing that manners differ in like people, that the British make more allowances for the Americans than vice versa, and that 'recent' people are crude, thin-skinned, self-conscious, and self-assertive, while a nation like England 'with a thousand years of greatness to her credit' has a thicker hide and can afford to be blunt. After all, England is the Lion, 'and we are her cub. She has often clawed us, and we have clawed her in return. This will go on.' On the charge of English 'land-grubbing', Wister reminds the Americans of their treatment of the Indians, and the hackneyed American question, 'What did England do in the war?' he answers by giving the true facts. He forgives even English arrogance, which is merely the seamy side of a just pride in a thousand years of tradition. 'She [England] is wise, far-seeing, less of an opportunist in her statesmanship than any other nation.'

The Austrian, Cohen-Portheim (*England, the Unknown Isle*, 1930) also refutes much of the universal criticism. He considers that the British genius for compromise, and ability to see two sides of a question—'not only . . . but also', 'on the one hand . . . on the other hand'—creates a happy mean on which other countries have to try to put their finger. For this reason the British nation is 'the least understood and the most grossly misrepresented in the world'.

Alfred Perlès' *Round Trip* (translated from *Aller Sans Retour London*, 1946) finds the British neither selfish nor mercenary, and imputes most misunderstanding of them to their sincerity and honesty. 'An Englishman means every word he says: that's why England is slandered, calumniated, criticized, denigrated all over the world.' He agrees they have no sense of humour, which is only possessed by real scoundrels. 'If the world is ever going to be initiated, in a massive, theophanic way, the initiation will come about by and through England.' Another great friend of England, Professor Commager, of New York, declares the English a 'decent folk', peaceful, generous and compassionate, and asserts that England 'still provides the world with a kind of moral Greenwich Line by which to measure all longitudes.'

No doubt English self-denigration has done something to perpetuate the clichés in foreign abuse. Carlyle asserts that the hell of the English soul is the 'terror of not succeeding, of not making money'. In a sermon in 1640 Thomas Fuller declares that 'Gluttony is the sin of England', but this admission was voiced by Ranulph Higden about 1350 ('they woneth to gluttony more than other men') and a British Museum manuscript (Harley 2252) of the time of Henry VIII even contains an *Apology for English Gluttony*. 'The most covetous and perfidious of mankind,' wrote Macaulay, a statement which, however, he did not invent. Swift contributed,

> He gave the little wealth he had,
> To build a house for Fools and Mad,
> And shew'd, by one satiric touch,
> No Nation wanted it so much.

Kipling said 'Allah created the English mad', and Mr Noël Coward plagiarized an alleged Indian wisecrack by singing about 'Mad dogs and Englishmen'. It may be that Hazlitt's Irish ancestry prompted the statement, in his 'English

Characteristics', that 'the English are the only people to whom the term *blackguard* is peculiarly applicable—by which I understand a reference of everything to violence and a contempt for the feelings and opinions of others', but the foreigner rarely distinguishes between English and British, and interprets this as self-criticism.

But the Englishman is not a little taken aback when his delicate parlour-game of self-depreciation is taken in deadly earnest by the literal-minded foreigner. 'That favourite topic of all intellectual Englishmen, the adverse criticism of things British' is usually either a peculiar and insular facet of the humour which foreigners deny the British even possess, or a weapon in the domestic game of politics. Misled by the stiff upper lip, and not noticing the tongue in cheek, the foreign observer solemnly concludes that a few discerning Englishmen are conscientiously reviewing the failings of their nation. Genet in 1757–9 published ten volumes in French translation of criticisms of England drawn from English tracts; Defoe's *Trueborn Englishman* was well-known abroad, and extracts were published in India in 1904 under the title of *John Bull's Failings*, and Addison's contributions to the *Spectator* appeared also in French. Thus England was assailed with her own homemade bombs. Byron's strictures on cant, the brutality depicted in Shakespeare and in novels like *Wuthering Heights*, the satiric presentation of English social life in almost all the nineteenth-century novelists, the enormous fund of self-caricature from Hogarth to *Punch*, and the stern animadversions of Opposition speakers in Parliament, have clearly offered a great deal of the ammunition. It is hardly surprising that Swift's 'pernicious race of little odious vermin' should have been a favourite quotation on the Continent, where he had such a great following.

Not only self-castigation but also British boasts, satirical and sober, have been taken and used in evidence against them, particularly caricatures in *Punch* depicting the assumption of English superiority, and discussions of English pre-eminence by English historians. And did not Milton, in his *Areopagitica*, remark that when God is decreeing to begin some new and great period in His church, 'What does He then do but reveal Himself to His servants, and as His manner is, first to His

49

Englishmen?' But no one has perhaps satirized this little failing better than the most English of novelists, Charles Dickens. 'This Island was Blest, Sir', said Mr Podsnap, 'to the Direct Exclusion of such Other Countries as—as there may happen to be. . . . There is in the Englishman a combination of qualities, a modesty, an independence, a responsibility, a repose, combined with an absence of everything calculated to call a blush into the cheek of a young person, which one would seek in vain among the Nations of the Earth.'

But the last word must be left with the tail-twisters. Few of them would be likely to agree with Pastor Wendeborn that the English, 'of all cultivated nations, approach the nearest to the character of what man, in reality ought to be', or the handsome tribute of Ambassador Walter Page (in a letter to Edward M. House, 1915), that 'the genuine, thorough-bred English man or woman is the real thing—one of the realest things in this world'. Alas, they would be unlikely to do more than echo the dictum of James Fenimore Cooper that England is a country 'that all respect, but few love'.

Tails

This one did not have a tail as the Englishman did.

> Nivardus of Ghent, *Isengrimus*, *c.* 1150

The English tale, or rather the English tail, was never upright and never deserved belief.

> Pierre Riga (?), *Causa regis Francorum contra regem Anglorum*, 1157–61

He [Raymond of Toulouse] has neither fear nor dread of these tailed English.

> Peire d'Auvergne, 1159

The Greeks and Sicilians called all those who followed that king 'English' and 'tailed'.

> Recorded by Richard of Devizes, *Chronicle*, *c.* 1191–2

The tailed English, born at their cups,
When they are drunk, they behave like beasts.

> Henry of Avranches, *Debate between Conradulus and an Englishman*, 1214–15

It is surprising that they [the women] do not blush to have tails on their dresses, seeing that the English blush to be called tailed.

> Etienne de Bourbon, 13th cent.

Being like to scorpions, the English are called tailed.
> A monk of Silly, *Pièce farcie*, 13th cent.

English boozers and tailed.
> Jacques de Vitry, *Historia Occidentalis*, 13th cent.

Englishman [*anglicus*], because he stings with his tail like a snake [*anguis*].
> Medieval Latin saying in France.

Since therefore thay have tails, it so happens that when they are angry they stiffen their tails; thus when angered, they cannot sit down.
> *Proprietates Anglicorum*, 14th cent.
> French MS. (T. Wright and J. O. Halliwell,
> *Reliquiae Antiquae*, 1843)

The English are stronger than the French. They carry two casks of beer on their backs and a tail behind.
> Eustaches Deschamps, late 14th cent.

Be gone, tail'd Englishmen, be gone!
Dame Fortune smiles on you no more.
Your banner, which so brightly shone,
Is now befoul'd with mud and gore.
Good Frenchmen, with sweet Joan before,
And fillèd all with heavenly fire,
Confounding you, your banner tore.
In truth, the news for you is dire.

In France shall justice now be done
To you, o'erproud since days of yore.
To us you seem mad, every one,
Who falsely sailed the Channel o'er.
Your just deserts you'll have and more:
Your banner trampled in the mire,
With flattened noses homeward pour.
In truth, the news for you is dire.

Just think of all under the sun,
Who stood by you in days before,
How now they everyone do shun
The sight of you for evermore.
Unless they be in travail sore,
No youth nor maid nor wife nor sire
Will succour you or you restore.
In truth, the news for you is dire.

And now your wages we will score:
May gout and gravel be your hire,
Your tails cut clean off to the core.
In truth, the news for you is dire.[1]

> Ballad against the English, 1429 (published
> P. Meyer, *Romania*, 1892)

After the tails! (i.e., After the English!)

> de Monstrelet, 1436

Thei clepyd hir Englisch sterte[2] & spokyn many lewyd wordys
vnto hir.

> *The Book of Margery Kempe*, 1436

We'll hear no more of these tailed English,
Cursed be the whole race.

> Anon. French poem in *Le Manuscrit de Bayeux*,
> 15th cent.

This nun cat comes from Calais,
Its mother was Cathau the Blue,
It must be of English extraction,
It has such a very long queue.

> Jean Molinet, *Le présent d'un cat nonne*, 1477

[Curtailing of Becket's sumpter-mule] And the good saint
made complaint of this and as a result, all the boys who have

---

[1] We have to thank Professor Armel Diverres for a prose translation of this poem
from medieval French. The doggerel is ours.
[2] = tail.

been born in that village until this day have come into the world with tails at their backs. This gave rise to the saying, which always much angers the English, 'Englishman, show me your tail.' And I would like to see anyone with the courage to go round that village calling out 'Tailed Englishman'.

Geschichte Wilwolts von Schaumburg, 1507

The Englishman has a tail behind,
He is therefore a dog.
O tailèd Englishman,
Take care of your tail,
Lest it fall off.
Because of the tail,
The English nation
Remains without honour.

George Dundas, Reply in Latin to John Skelton,
1513

Tailed goddams, amiable toads,
Go away and hide yourselves out of my sight.

Courroux de la Mort contre les Anglais, 1513

It is said that the English cut off the tail of St Thomas's horse, and that is why the English have short tails.

G. Paradin, *Anglicae Descriptionis
Compendium,* 1545

For you know that the English are depicted with a *queue derrière,* which means that they have an *arrière pensée* and a *garde derrière.*

Henry of Navarre to Beaumont, 1603

Abroad they take with them great trains of attendant servants, who wear their masters' arms in silver fastened to their left arms, and are justly teased that they have tails at their backs.

P. Hentzner, *Itinerarium Germaniae, Galliae,
Angliae* . . ., 1612 (transl. Earl of Orford, 1797)

And leave, with his tail,
His vain pride all despoiled.

Saint-Amant, *L'Albion*, 1644

If you call yourselves soldiers, do not hold your tails between your legs like panic-stricken dogs.

Joost van den Vondel, *Scheepskroon*, 1653

We thank you, O God, the only saviour of Holland, who have by your grace protected our fleets against the island of the godless, against the claws of griffins, so that they now run round in circles after their own tails from spite.

Henrik Brunô, *Danck-dicht aen Godt
almachtigh*, 1653

The Englishman is here called a Tailman, who seemed to be faithful and a good friend to everyone, but who stings and torments everyone cruelly so that they can hardly recover. Those who have a regard for truth are not sorry when the Tailman is called a bad man.

Herstelde See, 1654

Do not yield, Ruiter, to angels with tails.

de Kokerboer, poem to Michiel de Ruyter,
1658–9

The black or fallen angel[1] may caress the bear [i.e. the Swede] a little with his tail.

Oorloog in die Oostsee, 1658–9

But we know the habits of Leicester, who, in perjury and degeneration, stings everyone in the heart with his tail.

Joost van den Vondel, *Zeegevier der
Vrije Nederlanden op den Teems*, 1667

In France our 'tail' is good, our 'head' bad. . . . In England your 'head' is good, your 'tail' poor.

Napoleon, at Elba, to G. V. Vernon, Nov. 1814
(*see* J. H. Rose, *The Life of Napoleon I*, 1934)

---

[1] Pun on 'angels' and 'Angles'.

The Lion's Tail

An islander is an easily caught animal, especially the Englishman with his long tail of national arrogance and ignorance.

Bismarck to Leopold von Gerlach, 31.iii.1857

Everyone can see why the Lion should be a symbol for the British nation. This noble animal loves dignified repose. He haunts by preference solitary glades and pastoral landscapes. His movements are slow, he yawns a good deal; he has small squinting eyes high up in his head, a long displeased nose and a prodigious maw. He apparently has some difficulty in making things out at a distance as if he had forgotten his spectacles (for he is beginning to be an elderly lion now) but he snaps at the flies when they bother him too much. On the whole he is a tame lion: he has a cage called the Constitution, and a whole parliament of keepers with high wages and a cockney accent; and he submits to all the rules they make for him, growling only when he is short of raw beef. The younger members of the nobility and gentry may ride on his back and he obligingly lets his tail hang out of the bars, so that the little Americans and the little Irishmen and the little Bolshevists, when they come to jeer at him, may twist it.

G. Santayana, Soliloquies in England, 1922

The decrepit English lion . . . has now lost his tail in Egypt.

N. Khrushchev, 1957

Tweaks

You must look out in Britain that you are not cheated by the charioteers.

> Cicero to Trebatius, 54 B.C.

The Britons wholly sundered from all the world.

> Virgil, *Eclogues*, 37 B.C.

The Britons, no friends to strangers.

> Horace, *Odes*, c. 23 B.C.

They fight as individuals and are vanquished as a body.

> Tacitus, *Agricola*, A.D. 97–8

Nemo bonus Brito est.

> Ausonius, *Epigrams*, A.D. 370

Ferocious barbarians.

> Sidonius Apollinaris, 5th cent.

The British: according to some authorities so named because of their brutish character.

> Isidore, *Origines*, 622–33

Who dare compare the English, the most degraded of all the races under heaven, with the Welsh?

> Giraldus Cambrensis, 1204–5

61

Anglia, then *Anglicus* from *anda,* which means 'dung'.

> French attempt at etymology, no date

The English are best at weeping and worst at laughing.

> Medieval Latin proverb, no date

Le Comte de S.-Pol so hated the English that he could say nothing good of them.

> Froissart, *Chronicles,* late 14th cent.

An Englishman is a crook who cannot be trusted.
If he says 'hail' to you, beware of him as of an enemy.

> *Proprietates Anglicorum,* 14th cent.
> French MS. (see Wright and Halliwell)

God protect me from the treachery of the English.

> French MS. Ste Geneviève Library, 14th cent.

England, dregs of mankind, shame of the world, and the absolute end!

> *Disputatio inter Anglicum et Francum,*
> French, 1375-7 (?)

The English wear a naïve expression, and make promises, but you will never find one who will carry them out.

> *Dit de la Rebellion d'Engleterre,* 14th cent.

England, the heart of a rabbit in the body of a lion,
The jaws of a serpent, in an abode of popinjays.

> Eustache Deschamps, late 14th cent.

Then all who pass this way will say,
Here was once England.

> Eustache Deschamps, *De la prophécie Merlin sur la*
> *destruction d'Angleterre,* late 14th cent.

Englés borracho [the Englishman is a drunkard].

> Spanish saying, no date

Saoul comme un Anglois [drunk as an Englishman].
Proverbial (also Rabelais, 16th cent.)

O Englishman, Englishman, mend your ways: you promise
one thing and do another.
Alain Chartier, *Ballade de Fougères*, 1449

Every time I have to speak of the English, I cannot restrain
my pen from writing what it must.
Noel de Fribois, 1459

These drunken and infamous English.
La Folye des Anglois, late 15th cent.

Be gone, you foul creatures, gluttons, skunks, rotters,
Tailed goddams, so that I may never see you more.
Courroux de la Mort contre les Anglais, 1513

The men are more discreet in drinking than the Germans, but
more idle.
Mario Savorgnano, Venetian, 1531

A good country and a bad people.
Franco-Flemish proverb, 16th cent.

England,
Du Land der Schand',
Wie kommst du Satansland
Zum Namen Engelland?
[England, land of shame, how come you, land of
Satan, to the name of Angel-land?]
Old Hanseatic saying

Les Anglois séparez du monde.
Pierre de Ronsard, 1550

In all the four corners of the earth one of these three names is

given to him who steals from his neighbour: brigand, robber
or Englishman.

> *Les Triades de l'Anglais*, orig. Welsh, 1572,
> publ. French, 1890[1]

All these three live on blood: the flea, the mercenary, and the
Englishman.

> *ibid.*

Three things which only attack things weaker than themselves: the cat, the cormorant, and the Englishman.

> *ibid.*

England is the paradise of women, the purgatory of men, and
the hell of horses.

> John Florio, *Second Frutes*, 1591

They are good sailors, and better pirates, cunning, treacherous
and thievish.

> P. Hentzner, *Itinerarium Germaniae,*
> *Galliae, Angliae,* 1612

From England comes neither a good wind nor a good war.

> J. P. Masson, *Descriptio Fluminum*
> *Galliae,* 1618

The English are polite, but have false hearts.

> Juan Lorenzo, *El libro de Alexandre,* 1636

For me the English are amongst men as wolves amongst
animals.

> Guy Patin, 1649

L'Angleterre, ah! la perfide Angleterre.

> J. B. Bossuet, sermon, 1652

England is a little garden full of sour weeds.

> Louis XIV (attrib.) *c.* 1706

[1] There are 52 triads in all, one for each week of the year.

The English keep no mean, either in good or evil.
Louis de Muralt, Lettres sur les Anglois (1695),
1725

Englishmen are mighty swearers.
C. de Saussure, Lettres . . ., 1725

Ci-gît Jean Rosbif, escuyer,
Qui se pendit pour se désennuyer.
   [Here lies John Roast Beef, Esquire
   Who hanged himself to pass the time.]
P. Néricault-Destouches, early 18th cent.

In this country it is found requisite now and then to kill an admiral to encourage the others.
Voltaire, Candide, 1759

The gloomy Englishman, rationalizing even his love.
Voltaire, Les Originaux, c. 1760

English is a fine language: it is founded on 'God Damn'.
P. A. C. de Beaumarchais, Le Barbier de Séville,
1775

She [England] has been treacherous and we know it. Her character is gone and we have seen the funeral.
Thomas Paine, Common Sense, 29.10.1782
(see The American Crisis, 1792)

The English . . . will sacrifice their allies to peace, to further their own interests.
Frederick the Great, Die politischen Testamente,
1784

They have nothing in them to justify the ferocious pride which they manifest upon all occasions.
Mirabeau, letter, 1784

Love of eccentricity, which the English show on every possible occasion, no doubt prompts many of them to wear glasses.
F. W. von Schütz, *Briefe über London*, 1792

Exaggeration to the point of caricature is peculiar to the English nation.

ibid.

Let us attack and overthrow haughty Albion.
(*Another version:* Let us attack in her own waters Perfidious Albion.)
Augustin Ximénez, *L'Ère des Français*, 1793

Where is the nation, not only in Europe, but in the whole world, who has no accusation to make against these islanders?
Bertrand Barère, Report to the Convention, 1794

The lion of St Mark is no more; the eagle of the Caesars has been conquered; it only remains to destroy the British leopard.
Bertrand Barère, *La Liberté des Mers*, 1798

Every Englishman is an island.
Novalis, *Fragmente*, 1799

England itself has as many madmen, as many madhouses, as many books on madmen, as the rest of Europe put together.
Le peuple Anglais, bouffi d'orgeuil, de bière et de thé,
jugé au tribunal de la raison, 1803

I cannot bear red. It is the colour of England.
Napoleon (attrib.)

World-masters on the cheap.
Napoleon to Decrès, 1805 (*see* J. H. Rose,
The Life of Napoleon I, 1934)

A pirate spreading misery and ruin over the face of the ocean.
Thomas Jefferson to Walter Jones, 1810

In France the greatest disgrace is to lack courage: in England, to lack guineas.

> Jean-Baptiste Say, *De l'Angleterre et des Anglais*, 1815

The English have no exalted sentiments. They can all be bought.

> Napoleon to Gaspard Gourgaud, 1817

Money is highly prized in England; honour and virtue little.

> Montesquieu, *Notes sur l'Angleterre* (1729–32), 1818

The shoving propensities of the English.

> James Fenimore Cooper, *England, . . .*, 1837

The English—the most artificial people I know.

> *ibid.*

England, a land that all respect, but few love.

> *ibid.*

I buy glory as the Englishman buys love [said by Dauriat].

> H. de Balzac, *Illusions perdues*, 1837

Things they don't understand always cause a sensation among the English.

> Alfred de Musset, *Le Merle Blanc*, 1842

That mountain of shams.

> Margaret F. Ossoli to Emerson, 1846

As at Rome, so in England, they live by abuses; their interests, their traditions, render them hostile to progress.

> A. A. Ledru-Rollin, *De la Décadence de l'Angleterre*, 1850 (transl. 1850)

England is isolated, like the lone vulture in its eyrie.

> *ibid.*

Nobody is so perfect on all points — himself being the judge — as Bull.
Horace Greeley, Glances at Europe, 1851

The English are sharpers as a nation and honest as individuals.
E. L. A. and J. A. de Goncourt,
Le Journal des Goncourt, 29.x.1868

Englishmen are not made of polishable substance.
Nathaniel Hawthorne, Journal, 13.ii.1854

You enthuse with enraptured looks over the freedom of countries which possess no factories.
F. Grillparzer, Sprüche und Epigramme, 1854

England is the Promised Land of dilettantism.
Lothar Bucher, Der Parlamentarismus
wie er ist, 1855

The English shrink from a generalisation.
R. W. Emerson, English Traits, 1856

John Bull's Two Mottoes (for the present occasion, chiefly)
1. Necessity knows no law; and
2. Necessity is the Mother of Intervention!
Vanity Fair (New York), 26.vii.1862

In France, when one heard in the eighteenth century of anything harsh, low, ferocious, the remark was, 'How very English'.
A. Laugel, L'Angleterre politique et social,
1873 (transl. J. M. Hart, 1874)

I wouldn't change a dandy I know of for three young Englishmen.
F. Dostoevsky, The Brothers Karamazov, 1880

You English, like the Romans in many things, resemble them most in your ignorance of your own history.
Karl Marx to Hyndman, 1881

England is the home of shoddy.

> Max O'Rell [Paul Blouet], *John Bull and his Island*, 1883

The English have a love of pettifogging: it is in the Norman blood.

> *ibid.*

No people lose more time owing to want of method.

> Oliveira Martins, *A Inglaterra de Hoje*, 1892
> (transl. C. J. Willdey, 1896)

Money is the pride of the English.

> *ibid.*

Women, horses and money: these are the three idols of the British nature.

> *ibid.*

The English are, I think, the most obtuse and barbarous people in the world.

> Stendhal, *Souvenirs d'Egotisme*, 1892

The phenomenal bibulousness of the Briton.

> B. M. Malabari, *The Indian Eye on English Life*, 1893

An Englishman's friendship appears to be as fickle as his weather.

> *ibid.*

London! Dirty little pool of life.

> *ibid.*

The English are mentioned in the Bible: blessed are the meek, for they shall inherit the earth.

> Mark Twain, *Pudd'nhead Wilson's New Calendar*, 1893

The haughtiest flag that floats.

> J. J. Roche, *The Constitution's Last Fight*, 1895

The climate is on the side of the strong.

> E. Boutmy, *Essai d'une Psychologie politique du Peuple Anglais* . . ., 1901

Unmitigated noodles.

> Emperor Wilhelm II, 1901

British insolence and overbearing.

> *id.*, 1904

You British are mad, like bulls seeing a red flag.

> *id.*, 1908

In some ways they are incredibly far back in mediaevalism—incredibly.

> Ambassador Walter Page to Ed. M. House, 1914

Nothing is ever abolished, nothing ever changed.

> *id.* to the President, 1914

The Englishman is a traitor to civilization.

> A. von Harnack, Berlin speech, 1914

Gott strafe England.

> A. Funke, *Schwert und Mythe*, 1914

The cowardly old water-snake.

> L. Niessen-Deiters, 1915

England, the pious pirate.

> Count Ernst zu Reventlow, *Der Vampir des Festlandes*, 1915

Lying and hypocrisy in every page of England's history.

> A. Geiser, *Das perfide Albion*, 1915

John Bull would enrol gorillas in battalions if they could be trained.

> S. Gopčević, *Das Land der unbegrenzten
> Heuchelei*, 1915

No people has done so much harm to civilisation as the English.

> O. A. H. Schmitz, 1915 (*see* W. W. Coole
> and M. F. Potter, *Thus Spake Germany*, 1941)

The gentleman-cracksman of Conan Doyle expresses the soul of the nation.

> *ibid.*

England is the paradise of individuality, eccentricity, heresy, hobbies and humours.

> G. Santayana, *Soliloquies in England*, 1922

I know why the sun never sets on the British Empire: God wouldn't trust an Englishman in the dark.

> Duncan Spaeth, attrib.

I'm going to bust King George in the snoot—in Chicago.

> *Chicago Tribune*, April 1927

The British Empire has survived the hot joint and the cold potato and it can do anything.

> *ibid.*, 1.viii.1927

No Englishman's ever a gentleman when it comes to taking what he wants from a foreign country.

> G. H. Payne, *England: Her Treatment of America*,
> 1931 (quoting Trader Horn)

The world is inhabited by two species of human beings: mankind and the English.

> G. J. Renier, *The English: Are they Human?*, 1931

The public schools breed no Hamlets.

ibid.

Sex in England is considered a sinful thing, and is taboo.

ibid.

When an Englishman says 'I am afraid', he always means that he is damned sure.

C. Hansen, *The English Smile*, 1935

Sometimes it seems certain that they have kept their temperament down so long that they have smothered it.

ibid.

An Englishman will burn his bed to catch a flea.

Turkish proverbial saying, still current in 1936

Hypocrisy, thy name is England.

Westdeutscher Beobachter, March 1939

The English are not only unscrupulous politicians, but also bad soldiers.

Ribbentrop to Stalin, October 1940
(*Docs. on German Foreign Policy*, D. XI)

The English have never really invented anything original, but have always merely imitated what others did before them.

J. Goebbels, *Diary*, 18.iii.1943

The blindly groping Britisher, who prefers to trust his instincts rather than his intellect.

M. J. Bonn, *Wandering Scholar*, 1949

Thought, an affectation for the Englishman.

S. de Madariaga, *Portrait of Europe*, 1952

The English enjoy madness as a liberation from their usual objectivity.

ibid.

The British can be most unpleasant in a courteous way.
Emily Hahn, *Meet the British*, 1953

I was 17 before I knew that 'Damn British' was two words.
General Gruenther, speech, 8.vi.1954

The English are not a sculptural nation.
N. Pevsner, Reith Lecture, 1955

When an Englishman, especially an upper-class Englishman, desires to be rude, he makes the late Mr Vishinsky sound like a curate.
Drew Middleton, *The British*, 1957

You are still terrible snobs, with a caste system far more rigid than our own.
Mrs Pandit, interviewed by *Daily Mail*, July 1960

Twists

Appearance

They look like people crying for help.
Oliveira Martins, 1892

Lydia's morals are as loose as the ancient breeches of the poor Briton.
Martial, *Epigrams*, A.D. 98

Your faces are as ruddy as a dog's coat.
Eustache Deschamps, late 14th cent.

Noses like parrots and jaws like nutcrackers.
G. Casanova, 1763

The English have adopted the custom of dressing their hair almost against their will, and accordingly their friseurs are the most unskilful in Europe.
J. W. von Archenholz, *England und Italien*,
1785 (transl. 1789, 1791)

English beauty is more striking than attractive.
J. H. Meister, *Souvenirs d'un Voyage
en Angleterre*, 1791 (tr. 1799)

Englishwomen are not happy in their attire.
E. G. Geijer, *Impressions of England*, 1809–10
(transl. E. Sprigge and C. Napier, 1932)

An English grace reminds me irresistibly of the roast beef and wheaten bread.

ibid.

Quoique leur chapeaux soient bien laids,
Goddam! moi j'aime les Anglais!
   [Although their hats are so terribly ugly,
   God-damn! I love the English!]
                                        P. J. de Béranger, *Les Boxeurs*, 1814

The English ladies are imprisoned in stays, and in stays so stiff that to embrace them is like embracing an oak.
                              Count G. Pecchio, *Osservazioni semi-serie . . .,*
                                        1831 (transl. 1833)

It is the fault of their forms that they grow stocky, and the women have that disadvantage—few tall, slender figures of flowing shape, but stunted and thickset persons.
                              R. W. Emerson, *English Traits*, 1856

On emerging from the academy, they once more glanced round at the Englishmen, with long rabbit's teeth and drooping side-whiskers, who were walking behind them—and broke out laughing.
                              Ivan Turgenev, *On the Eve*, 1860

The physiognomy [of English ladies] is often pure, but also often sheepish. Many are simple babies, new waxen dolls, with glass eyes, which appear entirely empty of ideas. Other faces have become ruddy, and turned to raw beefsteak. There is a fund of folly, or of brutality in this inert flesh—too white or too red. Some are ugly or grotesque in the extreme; with heron's feet, stork's necks, always having the large front of white teeth, the projecting jaws of carnivora.
                              H. Taine, *Notes sur l'Angleterre*, 1871
                              (transl. W. F. Rae, 1872)

There is the same athletic and full-fleshed type among the gentlemen; I know four or five specimens among my acquaintances. Sometimes the excess of feeding adds a variety; this was true of a certain gentleman in my railway-carriage on the Derby day: large ruddy features, with flabby and pendent cheeks, large red whiskers, blue eyes without expression, an enormous trunk in a short light jacket, noisy respiration; his blood gave a tinge of pink to his hands, his neck, his temple, and even underneath his hair; when he compressed his eyelids, his physiognomy was as disquieting and heavy as that seen in the portraits of Henry VIII; when in repose, in presence of this mass of flesh, one thought of a beast for the butcher, and quietly computed twenty stones of meat. Towards fifty, owing to the effect of the same diet seasoned with port wine, the figure and the face are spoiled, the teeth protrude, the physiognomy is distorted, and turns to horrible and tragical caricature, as for example, a fat and fiery general at the Volunteer Review in Hyde Park, who had the air of a bull-dog and had a brick-dust face, spotted with violet excrescences. The last variety is seen among the common people, where spirits take the place of port, among other places in the low streets which border the Thames; several apoplectical and swollen faces, whereof the scarlet hue turns almost to black, worn-out, blood-shot eyes like raw lobsters; the brute brutalised. Lessen the quantity of blood and fat, while retaining the same bone and structure, and increasing the countrified look: large and wild beard and moustache, tangled hair, rolling eyes, truculent muzzle, big knotted hands; this is the primitive Teuton issuing from his woods; after the overfed animal, comes the fierce animal, the English bull.

ibid.

One is struck by the number of faces which exhibit this type of cold and determined will. They walk straight, with a geometrical movement, without looking on either hand; without distraction, wholly given up to their business, like automatons, each moved by a spring; the large bony face, the pale complexion, often sallow or leaden-hued, the rigid look, all, even to their tall, perpendicular black hat, even to the strong and large foot-covering, even to the umbrella rolled in its case and carried in a particular style, display the man unsensitive, dead to ideas of pleasure and elegance, solely preoccupied in getting through much business well and rapidly.

ibid.

On a journey, I have seen Englishmen supplied with so many glasses, opera-glasses and telescopes, with so many um-brellas, canes and iron-tipped sticks; with so many overcoats, comforters, waterproofs and wrappers; with so many dressing-cases, flasks, books, and newspapers, that were I in their place I should have stayed at home.[1]

ibid.

An Englishwoman is seldom handsome after thirty.

Max O'Rell [Paul Blouet], *John Bull
and his Island*, 1883

His hat is as sacred to an Englishman as his beard is to a Mussulman.

O. Wendell Holmes, sen., *Our Hundred
Days in Europe*, 1887

The mournful eyes and prim lips of the English.

Stendhal, *Souvenirs d'Egotisme*, 1892

John Bull, the type of Punch's caricatures, cannot be said to be the representative of the Londoners of the present day. John Bull remained provincial. When the buds in the bouquet of flowers unfold they produce a different kind of creature. The infant made of milk and roses, that used to develop into a bull-dog's face over a stout cattle-salesman's body, pot-bellied and in Wellington boots, in an attitude insolently heavy, becomes, now that half-a-century of universal power and incomparable riches have had their effect upon the race, a type more lively, more agile, more graceful. More sym-pathetic? I do not know. It is less pleasant. The expression of

---

[1] In 1860 Capt. G. V. Macdonald, a British subject, was actually arrested in Bonn and jailed on a charge of trying to reserve several seats with his luggage in a railway carriage, and resisting the guard who objected (see *The Times*, 23.x. 1860, quoting the *National-Zeitung*).

the eyes, fixed and shining like those of cats, announces the ferocious character of modern life, foreign to the repose and stability of former times, in which John Bull worked calmly as a farmer upon his own land without any care. Now he has to live through the whirlwind of the town: he has to become industrial, giving himself up, in the great country of men, to hunting the hare that he calls a sovereign, under pain of being thrown on one side like a rag upon the dust-heap of human misery. The intensity of life reacts upon the anatomy of the body. John Bull *has become an American*. But he has not on this account lost the more striking lines of his physiognomy, the short neck, the large jaw-bone of the powerful masticator, the lively eye with the thick eyebrows announcing the animal spirits in his choleric temperament. The fleshy profile with large upper lip, the regular mark of the heavy intelligence always seen in the air of suppression on the countenance and in the facility of expression of wonderment. It may be said that the Englishman is in a chronic condition of being startled.

Oliveira Martins, *A Inglaterra de Hoje*,
1892 (transl. C. J. Willdey, 1896)

[Beauty of misses—transitory] Under the velvety skin hard bones are growing. The faces little by little assume a cutting expression. . . . Superfluity has withered them up, and as their beauty was not geometric, unpromising physiognomies have begun to design themselves. The air cuts their skin; their faces shrivel with veins and hard lines, their noses either get as sharp as razors, or assume the colour of tomatoes. Sometimes they call to mind raw beef, at other times under their reddish hair, more or less dyed, they seem vine-leaves tinged by an autumn sun. Their mouths grow ugly; the teeth, growing forward, attack one carnivorously. The feet at times attain the limits of grotesque ugliness, suspended on legs like poles; while the necks get as lanky as drakes! They look like people crying for help, and one recognises the propriety with which Garrett divided humanity into 3 sexes: masculine, feminine, and old English-women.

ibid

The complexions of the English have often been exploited for our benefit. The damp climate and the exercise out-of-doors produce the red, they say. But on examination it proves not to be the red of the rose, but the red of raw beef, and often streaky and fibrous at that. The features are large and the faces high-coloured, but it is not a delicate pink, it is a coarse red. At a distance the effect is charming, bright, refreshing, but close to, often rather unpleasant. Here the features of the women, even the features of the beautiful women, are moulded; while the features of our beautiful American women are chiselled.

> Price Collier, *England and the English*, 1909

Equally little could Motley have meant that the diners were good to look at. Nothing could be worse than the toilettes; nothing less artistic than the appearance of the company. One's eyes might be dazzled by the family diamonds, but, if an American woman was present, she was sure to make comments about the way the jewels were worn. If there was a well-dressed lady at table, she was either an American or 'fast'. She attracted as much notice as though she were on the stage. No one could possibly admire an English dinner-table.

> Henry Adams, *The Education of Henry Adams*,
> 1918 (privately pr., 1907)

. . . the perennial puzzle of an Englishman's face that guards the secret of a soul like a sphinx before a temple where mysterious rites are celebrated.

> G. J. Renier, *The English: Are they Human?*, 1931

Every Englishman wears a mackintosh, and has a cap on his head and a newspaper in his hand.

> Karel Čapek, *Letters from England*, 1932

Nature here has a propensity for unusual shagginess, excrescences, woolliness, spikiness, and all kinds of hair; English horses, for example, have regular tufts and tassels of hair on their legs, and English dogs are nothing more nor less than

5 Truth Fettered – John Bull's First Deed of Heroism.
Lies, Nothing but Lies, *Kladderadatsch, England-Album*, 1917

6 The English Traveller Abroad, *L'Assiette au Beurre*, January 1903

absurd bundles of forelocks. Only the **English lawn and** the English gentleman are shaved every day.

ibid.

Englishwomen's shoes look as if they had been made by someone who had often heard shoes described, but had never seen any, and the problem of buying shoes in London is almost insoluble—unless you pay a staggering tariff on American ones. What provokes this outburst is that I have just bought a pair of English bedroom slippers and I not only cannot tell the left foot from the right, but it is only after profound deliberation that I am able to distinguish between the front and the back.

M. Halsey, *With Malice toward Some*, 1938

In America, if a woman appeared at dinner in a dress which was a mass of wrinkles, people would raise their eyebrows and assume that she had just come from being tumbled in a haymow; but in England that haymow look is a sign of the purest and most incontestable virtue.

ibid.

Why are the false teeth so amateurish? They all look as though they had been filched from the Etruscan room of a museum.

ibid.

With the first nip in the October air the English bleakly begin fossicking around their wardrobes to assemble their collections of shapeless gruel-coloured outer garments, which will be worn for the next seven months straight. This is only grim resignation at the prospect of prolonged rain, snow, cold and sleet.

Sydney Sun, 7.x.1954

Character

*Angli perfidi, inflati, feri, contemptatores, stolidi,
amentes, inertes inhospitales, immanes.*
Scaliger, 1561

In England Pride has married his three daughters, Envy, Lust
and Sloth.
Guillaume Le Clerc of Normandy, *c.* 1225

Though they are circumspect in action and physically strong,
yet they are mentally defective. Therefore they need to employ
treachery in order to finish what they have begun.
Proprietates Anglicorum, 14th cent.
French MS. (publ. T. Wright and J. O.
Halliwell, *Reliquiae Antiquae*, 1843)

The Englysshe men were so prowde that they set nothyng by
ony nacyon but by theyr owne.
Froissart, *Chronicles*, transl. Lord Berners,
late 14th cent.

They are the peryloust people of the worlde, and most outragyoust if they be up, and specially the Londoners.
ibid.

In you there is nought but inconstancy:
Envy, pride, lust and lies.
Without fear of God or true affection,
Poltroons, cowards, skulkers and dastards.
Eustache Deschamps, late 14th cent.

Return to the beer on which you have all been nourished, you gross, leprous, stinking, corrupt creatures. We shall humble and overthrow your great pride, as surely as death comes to all.

> Anon. French ballad addressed to the
> English, 1441

The English are, in my opinion, perfidious and cunning, plotting the destruction of the lives of foreigners, so that, even if they humbly bend the knee, they cannot be trusted.

> Leo de Rozmital, travels of (Schasek's
> account), *c.* 1465–7

The King has the greatest desire to employ foreigners in his service. He cannot do so; for the envy of the English is diabolical, and, I think, without equal.

> Ayala to Ferdinand and Isabella, 1498

The English are of very changeable character, and it is difficult to negotiate with them.

> De Puebla to Ferdinand and Isabella, 1498

The English are great lovers of themselves, and of everything belonging to them . . . and whenever they see a handsome foreigner, they say that 'he looks like an Englishman', and that 'it is a great pity that he should not be an Englishman'.

> A. Trevisano, *A Relation . . . of the Island
> of England, c.* 1500

They would sooner give five or six ducats to provide an entertainment for a person, than a groat to assist him in any distress.

> *ibid.*

They have an antipathy for foreigners, and imagine that they never come into their island, but to make themselves masters of it, and to usurp their goods; neither have they any sincere and solid friendships amongst themselves, insomuch that they do not trust each other to discuss either public or private affairs together, in the confidential manner we do in Italy. And although their dispositions are somewhat licentious, I have never noticed anyone, either at court or amongst the lower orders, to be in love; whence one must necessarily conclude, either that the English are the most discreet lovers in the world, or that they are incapable of love. I say this of the men, for I understand that it is quite the contrary with the women, who are very violent in their passions. Howbeit the English keep a very jealous guard over their wives, though everything may be compensated in the end, by the power of money.

ibid.

Aimable comme un Anglais.

French proverbial saying, 16th cent.

You never kept faith with any man. Many times you have caused to die in great confusion your lord and king, so that you are known in all the world as the most faithless of races.

Nunc Dimittis des Anglais, 1543 (but possibly earlier and revived)

The perfidious, haughty, savage, disdainful, stupid, mad, slothful, inhospitable, inhuman English.

J. C. Scaliger, *Poetices*, 1561

Neere approaching to them [Italians] in quality (but yet somewhat differing) are Englishmen: who being of heat more weake and less boyling (as the which is well entermedled, overcome and qualified by moistnesse) are of stature comely and proportionable, and of body lusty and well complexioned: But to the studies of humanity, not so greatly given, and in exquisite arts not so well furnished. . . . And because they have somewhat thicke spirits, slenderly perfused with heat, they will stomacke a matter vehemently, and a long time lodge an inward grudge in their hearts, whereby it hapneth that when their rage is up, they will not easily be pacified, neither can their high and haughty stomackes lightly bee conquered, otherwise then [*sic!*] by submission, and yeelding to their minde and appetite onely.

> L. Lemnius, *The Touchstone of Complexions*
> (Latin 1561, transl. by T. Newton, 1581)

The people are bold, courageous, ardent and cruel in war, fiery in attack, and having little fear of death; they are not vindictive, but very inconstant, rash, vainglorious, light and deceiving, and very suspicious, especially of foreigners, whom they despise.

> E. van Meteren, *Nederlandtsche Historie*, 1599
> (*see* W. B. Rye, *England as seen by Foreigners*, 1865)

They are vastly fond of great noises that fill the ear, such as the firing of cannon, drums, and the ringing of bells, so that it is common for a number of them, that have got a glass in their heads, to go up into some belfrey, and ring the bells for hours together for the sake of exercise. If they see a foreigner very well made, or particularly handsome, they will say, *It is a pity he is not an Englishman*.

> P. Hentzner, *Itinerarium Germaniae, Galliae, Angliae*, 1612 (transl. Earl of Orford, 1797)

There is no nation in Europe more haughty, more insolent, more intoxicated with the idea of its own importance. According to them, wit and good judgment are only found in England. They worship their own opinions and despise those of every other nation.

> Duc de Sully, *Mémoires*, 1638

Consider what they call principles of government; you will find only laws of pride, adopted out of arrogance or sloth.

> *ibid.*

In short, the Englishman is a simpleton, so accustomed to hanging, that at the first sickness he imagines, he hangs himself on the rafters of his house.

> Saint-Amant, *L'Albion*, 1644

It used to be the abode of angels and saints, but is now the hell of demons and parricides. But for all that, it has not changed its nature, . . . and just as in hell the justice of the All-powerful is accompanied by pity, so in this execrable island you will find vestiges of bygone piety, and the stirrings and overthrow of the brutality and superstition of a mad, though stupid and northern nation.

> L. Coulon, *Le Fidèle Conducteur pour le Voyage d'Angleterre*, 1654

This speed, they make on Horseback, appeared so much the more remarkable to me, because of its been used in a Country where the People are very lazy, which I can very well affirm without Offence; for they do perhaps glory in their Sloth, and believe that true living consists in their knowing how to live at Ease.

> S. de Sorbière, *Voyage en Angleterre*, 1663 (transl. J. Woodward, 1709)

For as they are naturally lazy, and spend half their Time in taking Tobacco, they are all the time exercising their Talents about the Government, talking of new Customs, of the Chimney-Money, the management of the Publick Treasure, and the Lessening of Trade.

> *ibid.*

But the *English* may be easily brought to anything, provided you fill their Bellies, let them have freedom of speech, and do not bear too hard upon their lazy Temper.

> *ibid.*

The Common people of London, giving way to their natural inclination, are proud, arrogant, and uncivil to foreigners, against whom, and especially the French, they entertain a great prejudice and cherish a profound hatred, treating such as come among them with contempt and insult.

> L. Magalotti, *Travels of Cosmo III, Grand Duke of Tuscany . . .*, *1669* (transl. 1821)

The English are violent in their passions and do not try to restrain them. . . . When they fall in love they marry without much thought and without regard to the state of their affairs. That is why they are considered so suitable for establishing colonies.

> G. L. Le Sage, *Remarques sur l'État présent*
> *d'Angleterre . . . dans les années 1713 et 1714*, 1715

I think that those who accuse the English of being cruel, envious, distrustful, vindictive and libertine, are wrong. It is true that they take pleasure in seeing gladiators fight, in seeing bulls torn to pieces by dogs, seeing cocks fight, and that in the carnivals they use batons against the cocks, but it is not out of cruelty so much as coarseness.

> *ibid.*

Like fickle Proteus a hundred times
They change their moods, beliefs and minds;
And even within a single day
One finds them dreamy, sad or gay.

> A. F. Boureau Deslandes, *Nouveau Voyage*
> *d'Angleterre*, 1717

They look on foreigners in general with contempt, and think nothing is as well done elsewhere as in their own country.

> C. de Saussure, *Lettres et Voyages . . . 1725-9*,
> 1903 (transl. Mme van Muyden, 1902)

At Portsmouth I learned to know English naval officers. Good Lord! What men! I found to my cost that the greater number were the most debauched, the most dissolute, and the most terrible swearers I had ever come across.

> *ibid.*

The ordinary Amusements of the *English* are, Wine, Women, and Dice, or, in a Word, Debauchery. They are not nice at least in the two first, which they join together, without either Delicacy or Agreeableness: One may say that they drink for drinking sake, and their *Whores* must drink after the same

Manner, and they are highly pleas'd to find any that can keep up with them. These Debauches continue a long time, and are sometimes carryed very far.

L. de Muralt, *Lettres sur les Anglois*, 1725
(transl. 1726)

Corruption is come to such a heighth in *England*, that it appears barefaced. I have sometimes heard people impute it to King Charles II, who is reported to have given continual Examples of Excess and Debauchery; but in my Opinion, the *English* don't stand in need of any extraordinary Precedents, to make them what they are: Generally speaking, they have little Education, a great deal of money to lavish, and all possible Incentives to vice.

ibid.

If I durst, I would readily say, that there's a strong Resemblance between the *English* and their Dogs. Both are silent, head-strong, lazy, unfit for Fatigue, no way quarrelsome, intrepid, eager in fight, insensible of blows, and incapable of parting.

ibid.

He hates Difficulties and working, and thinks himself unhappy when he is engaged in Things of that kind; he is disheartened at such as are tedious, and resolves immediately to cut out what he finds troublesome to unravel. He is credulous in what does not much concern him, and to save the trouble of examining, easily believes everything that is reported, which I believe is the Reason we hear so much talk of apparitions in this Country. . . . When they lay Reason aside (which happens sometimes) they quite run away from it and then of all Men they are the least reasonable. They are violent in their Desires, impatient in ill Fortune, and little capable of finding a Remedy; furious in Anger, to a Degree of beating their Faces with their Fists, which they do sometimes on trifling Occasions, and on greater, proceed to more violent Resolutions.

ibid.

The English, not content with the preference they give them-selves over their neighbours, do not even take the pains to disguise their contempt for some of them, and their hatred of others.

J. B. Le Blanc, *Lettres d'un François*, 1745
(transl. 1747)

This sad disposition of their minds is perhaps the cause, which makes them so violent in their passions: they eagerly pursue the object which diverts them from it: and thus they exhaust themselves and not only become early insensible to the pleasure of life, but unable to bear misfortunes of ever so short duration.

ibid.

The *Parfait Anglais*, journeying without aim,
Buying at fabulous cost his new 'antiques',
Regarding all he sees with proud disdain,
Despising all the saints and their reliques.

Voltaire, *La Pucelle*, 1755

The chief characteristic of these haughty islanders is their national pride which makes them place themselves far above other nations.

G. J. Casanova de Seingalt, 1763
(*see Mémoires*, 1826–38)

[Says he had] *un véritable spleen britannique.*

ibid.

The Baron has returned from England: he came back dissatisfied . . . with the aristocrats who are gloomy, cold, proud, haughty and vain, and the commoners who are hard, insolent and uncouth.

D. Diderot to Mlle Volland, 1765

All that I find reprehensible in the general character of the English . . . is, a certain insensibility, which in the common people sometimes proceeds to ferocity, and which even reigns in their very pleasures. Such as the murdering chace; the baiting of bulls and other animals; their races, in which both men and horses somtimes perish; the brutal combats between the men themselves, and other things of the same kind. The English not only see all these barbaritys without emotion, but even pay for the pleasure of seeing them. I am inclined to think that the climate, their method of living, especially among the marine, ancient custom, wrong education, and other causes, either physical or moral, must have given this insensibility to the English.

> J. F. von Bielfeld, *Letters*, transl. W. Hooper, 1768–70 (letter 10.v.1741)

The laws against suicide have not been able to conquer the habit amongst the English.

> P. J. Grosley, *Londres*, 1770

The next day, in a squalid, ill-furnished, ill-served and ill-lit coffee-house, I found most of the gentlemen who, the day before, had been so pleasant and affable; none of them gave the slightest sign of recognition. I attempted to draw one or two into conversation, but could get no reply at all, or at the most, a mere 'yes' or 'no', and I began to think that something I had said the day before had offended them. I searched my mind, and tried to remember whether I had extolled the products of Lyons above theirs, or if I had said that the French cuisine was superior to the English, that Paris was a pleasanter town than London, that one could enjoy life better at Versailles than St James's, or some other dreadful faux-pas. But finding no fault with my conversation of the previous day, I took the liberty of asking one of them in a lively way that they seemed to find very strange, why they all looked so sad. He suddenly replied that the wind was in the east. At that moment one of their friends came in and said with a complete lack of expression, 'Molly cut her throat this morning. Her lover found her dead in her room with a blood-stained razor beside her.' This Molly was a young, beautiful and very rich young lady, on the point of getting married to the young man who had found her dead. These gentlemen, who were all friends of hers, received the news without even wincing. One of them merely asked what had become of her lover. *He has bought the razor*, replied one of the company dispassionately.

I myself, shocked by so strange a death and the indifference of these men at the news, could not help asking why a young lady like that, apparently so happy, should take her life in this cruel fashion: the only answer I got was that the wind was in the east.

> Voltaire, *Projet d'une lettre sur les Anglais,*
> publ. 1785

The excessive moroseness and unsociable temper of the English must be attributed to their extreme eagerness to read those immense quantities of Gazettes and political papers which are printed every day.

It is often with the greatest difficulty that you can prevail on an Englishman to speak; his answer is seldom more than *yes* or *no*: but if one has the address to turn the subject upon politics, his face immediately brightens up, he opens his mouth, and becomes eloquent.

> J. W. von Archenholz, *England und Italien,*
> 1785 (transl. 1789, 1791)

Would one believe it, that in a country where people swear at every word, where oaths make a part of the gallantry peculiar to sailors, and the lower ranks, swearing is expressly prohibited by law?

> *ibid.*

In England animals are treated with almost as much humanity as though they were rational beings.

> *ibid.*

How ingenious soever the English may be in evading a law which operates to their disadvantage they are always sufficiently careful not to infringe it directly.

> *ibid.*

The greatest preference which an Englishman gives to his island is, in my opinion, owing to the education he has received, so different from that in other countries: to the diet and manners he is used to, peculiar to his native soil: and above all, because he is told from his infancy that England is superior to all other countries, and that none are comparable to it.

G. F. A. Wendeborn, *A View of England . . .*, 1791

Madness seems to be more at home in England than in other countries.

ibid.

Haughty lords of the main, who are as gloomy as the mists which hang over the element of your glory. . . . Ye may be men of understanding, but ye are very dull and tedious companions.

N. Karamzin, *Travels . . . through Prussia . . .
and England*, 1791 (in Russian), transl. 1803

And above all, selfishness, greed, envy, anger, brutality and the like replace the love of honour, unselfishness, kindness, charity, friendship and respect for others which are found in better nations.

A. Riem, *Reise durch England*, 1798–9

In the eyes of the Englishman the Frenchman is a dog, the Spaniard a fool, the German a drunkard, the Italian a bandit. . . . Only the Englishman is the *non plus ultra* of perfection, and Nature's masterpiece.

ibid.

The abysmal pride of the Englishman or the stubbornness always attendant upon ignorance, will not allow him to stoop to imitation. . . . He always wanted to be original, and so goes on copying himself, remaining thus on the low cultural level on which we find him.

ibid.

And it is an everlasting truth that no nation on God's earth could be more corrupt, more wallowing in gluttony and debauchery and consequently more uncouth and lacking in all refinement both of mind and feeling, than the nation which squanders in one single night 10 million gilders, and therefore in a year 3,650 million gilders in swilling, whoring and other debauchery. And how the oft trumpeted good deeds of the few righteous amongst these people seem a mere nothing in comparison! And is not British greatness compared with British corruption, British generosity compared with British debauchery, as a mere drop is to a vessel of water?

ibid.

I know of no cultured nation in Europe whose thoughts and actions rest on less solid foundations than those of the English. They lack that universally prized talent of constancy, which presupposes a firm basis of ideas. Proof of this is their tendency to fickleness, their surprising curiosity, their amazement at the sight of unfamiliar things; the readiness with which they abandon their principles; the recklessness with which they will wager honour, fortune, prosperity and domestic happiness and risk it in a game of chance; their vacillation in matters of taste; their liking for oddness, often to the extent of caricature, and the stamp of madness, which characterises them more than any other nation in the world, and does not desert them even in their last hour.

ibid.

One might say that the Englishman puts into manual labour the delicacy that we put into that of the mind.

F. R. de Chateaubriand, *De l'Angleterre et des Anglais*, publ. *Mercure de France*, 5.vii.1801

The principal fault of the English is pride.

ibid.

It is always in autumn that the English malady, or the desire to commit suicide, appears.

Le peuple Anglais, bouffi d'orgeuil, de bière et de thé, jugé au tribunal de la raison, 1803

[quoting from M. Baert] Pride and covetousness are . . . the chief traits of the English character.

ibid.

We hear of national habits. Oh! those strange habits of a country overrun with brigandage, a country where conscience, honesty and convictions are bought and sold like commodities; a country where a man may attach a cord to his wife's neck and sell her in the market for a few shillings.

ibid.

England is distinguished as the country in which the greatest number of suicides are committed.

Mme de Stael, *Reflections on Suicide*, 1813

It is related of an Englishman that he hanged himself, to avoid the daily task of dressing and undressing.

J. W. von Goethe, *Dichtung und Wahrheit*, Book 13, 1814

It is cowardly to commit suicide. The English often kill themselves—it is a malady caused by the humid climate.

Napoleon, recorded by Gourgaud, 1817

All Englishmen are, as such, without reflection, properly so-called; distractions and party spirit will not permit them to perfect themselves in quiet.

J. W. von Goethe, recorded by J. P. Eckermann, *Gespräche mit Goethe . . . 1823–32*, 1836–48

In England, on the contrary, habits and prejudices hold such sway over men's minds that, with few exceptions, they are become incapable of reasoning in any concatenation of ideas out of their usual course. And even the most enlightened men are much more ready to seek arguments in defence of what exists among them, than impartially to examine what is most desirable for the physical and moral welfare of the human species.

A. de Stael-Holstein, *Lettres sur l'Angleterre*, 1825 (transl. 1830)

The taste of the English for titles and aristocratic distinctions is carried to a foolish excess. You will see them rush in crowds

97

to stare at a foreign prince, whose fortune and importance are inferior to the least member of the house of commons.

ibid.

[On advertising] The English, so simple in their manners, so taciturn and circumspect in their conversation, have recourse on these occasions to a superfluity of bombastic puffs, that would not disgrace the eloquence of a quack in the public square of Naples. This practice is so common, that it has even received a particular name, *the art of puffing*.

ibid.

In no country was selfishness more omnipotent; no people were perhaps less essentially humane in their political or in their private relations.

J. W. von Goethe, 1826, related by H. Fürst von Pückler-Muskau in *Briefe eines Verstorbenen*, 1831

The individual Englishman does not, in all cases, recommend his country; and the Englishman who travels without having learnt to curb his national pride, and his prejudices against everything which is not English, . . . the Englishman who emerges without being a little polished from that rust which is the native varnish of all islanders, of all people riveted to their inveterate habits, and which John Bull regards as the glory and perfection of his national character and of his patriotism: —such an Englishman is certainly not the most engaging sample of his country.

J. C. Beltrami, *A Pilgrimage in Europe and America*, 1828

Nowhere are there so many hypocrites as in England.

J. W. von Goethe, 1828, reported by F. Förster

There are today in London fifteen hundred thousand souls, if you can call the egoists who live there 'souls'.

Talleyrand to Mme Adelaide, 2.x.1830

First of all, said Julien, the wisest Englishman is mad for an

GORILLA BRITANNICUS.

IE STOOD THERE, AND BEAT HIS BREAST WITH HIS HUGE FISTS, TILL IT SOUNDED LIKE AN IMMENSE BASS DRU
ANTIME GIVING VENT TO ROAR AFTER ROAR. (*Du Chaillu.*)

7 Gorilla Britannicus, *Vanity Fair* (New York) 1862

L'Assiette au Beurre

40 Centimes

LES ANGLAIS
CHEZ NOUS

par Sancha

NGLAIS. — Un
eur qui gêne les
chez lui, mais qui
gêne pas chez les

tionnaire de l'Académie.)

8 The English in France, *L'Assiette au Beurre*, January 1903

hour every day; he is visited by the demon of suicide, who is the national deity. Secondly, intelligence and genius lose twenty-five per cent of their value on landing in England.

> Stendhal, *Le Rouge et le Noir*, 1831

It is an almost universal weakness of the unnoble in England to parade an acquaintance with the noble.

> [H. Fürst von Pückler-Muskau], *Briefe eines Verstorbenen*, 1831

This indifference to the feelings of others is a dark spot on the national manners of England.

> J. Fenimore Cooper, *England, . . .*, 1837

From every Englishman emanates a kind of gas, the deadly choke-damp of boredom.

> H. Heine, *Ludwig Börne*, 1840

That vile land where machines behave like men and men like machines.

> *ibid.*

But this time my joy at returning is doubled, for I have left England. Yes, I say England, although I did not actually cross the Channel. I spent four weeks in Boulogne, already an English town. It is full of Englishmen, and one hears nothing but English from morning till night; alas, even until well into the night, if one is unfortunate enough to have fellow lodgers who talk politics until the small hours over their tea and grog. For four weeks I heard nothing but those hissing sounds of the egoism which is manifest in every syllable and every intonation of their speech. . . . The masses, these typical Englishmen—God forgive me—repel me to the depths of my soul, and sometimes I find it impossible to look upon them as my fellow beings; instead they seem to me like odious automatons, machines propelled by egoism. Then I can almost hear the whirring wheels, with which they think, feel, count, digest and pray—their praying, their mechanical Anglican

church-going with their gilded prayer-books under their arms,
their dull and tedious Sunday, their clumsy affection of piety I
find most repulsive of all. I am firmly convinced that a
blaspheming Frenchman is a more pleasing sight than a praying Englishman. At other times these Englishmen remind me
of a grim spectre, and I find these thick-set, red-faced ghosts,
walking about perspiring in the fiercest sunlight, far more
creepy than the pale phantoms of the ghostly midnight hour.
And their complete lack of manners! With their angular limbs
and stiff elbows they push their way everywhere, and never
utter a single word of apology. And how hateful these red-
haired barbarians, eating their underdone beef, must appear to
the Chinese, who are born polite, and who, as we know, spend
two-thirds of their day practising this national virtue.

H. Heine, *Lutezia*, 1842

This contempt for foreigners is a feeling which the intelligent
people seek to conceal under the common cloak of politeness,
and which the lower classes express with the utmost coarseness.

L. Faucher, *Études sur l'Angleterre*, 1845

The distinguished Englishman has something which is akin to
the aristocracy of the beautiful and kindly dogs of his country.

E. L. A. and J. A. de Goncourt, *Le Journal*
des Goncourt, 1851–70

Every man in this polished country consults only his convenience, as much as a solitary pioneer in Wisconsin. I know
not where any personal eccentricity is so freely allowed, and no
man gives himself any concern with it. An Englishman walks
in a pouring rain, swinging his closed umbrella like a walking-
stick; wears a wig or shawl, or a saddle, stands on his head, and
no remark is made. And as he has been doing this for several
generations it is now in the blood.

In a company of strangers you would think him deaf: his
eyes never wander from his table and newspaper. He is never
betrayed into any curiosity or unbecoming emotion. They have
all been trained in one severe school of manners, and never put

off the harness. He does not give his hand. He does not let you meet his eye. It is almost an affront to look a man in the face, without being introduced. In mixed or in select companies they do not introduce persons; so that a presentation is a circumstance as valid as a contract. Introductions are sacraments. He withholds his name. At the hotel he is hardly willing to whisper it to the clerk at the book-office.

R. W. Emerson, English Traits, 1856

A slow temperament makes them less rapid and ready than other countrymen, and has given occasion to the observation, that English wit comes afterwards – which the French denote as *esprit d'escalier*.

ibid.

They have no curiosity about foreigners, and answer any information you may volunteer with 'Oh, Oh!' until the informant makes up his mind that they shall die in their ignorance, for any help he will offer. There are really no limits to this conceit, though brighter men among them make painful efforts to be candid.

ibid.

There is no country in which so absolute a homage is paid to wealth. In America, there is a touch of shame when a man exhibits the evidences of large property, as if, after all, it needed apology. But the Englishman has pure pride in his wealth, and esteems it a final certificate.

ibid.

The French say that Englishmen in the street always walk straight before them like mad dogs.

ibid.

The bias of England to practical skill has reacted on the national mind.

ibid.

The habit of brag runs through all classes, from *The Times* newspaper through politicians and poets, through Wordsworth, Carlyle, Mill and Sydney Smith, down to the boys of Eton.

ibid.

An Englishman who has lost his fortune, is said to have died of a broken heart. The last term of insult is 'a beggar'.

ibid.

Of all the sarse that I can call to mind,
England *doos* make the most unpleasant kind:
It's you're the sinner ollers, she's the saint;
Wut's good's all English, all thet isn't ain't.

J. Russell Lowell, *The Biglow Papers*,
Second Series, 1862

When we scratch the covering of an Englishman's morality, the brute appears in all its violence and ugliness.

H. Taine, *Hist. de la Litt. Anglaise*, 1863–4

Everyone is drunk, but drunk joylessly, gloomily and helplessly, and everyone is somehow strangely silent. Only curses and bloody brawls occasionally break that suspicious and depressing silence.

F. Dostoevsky, *Zimnia Zamietki* . . .
(*Summer Impressions*), 1863

In London you no longer see the populace. Instead you see a loss of identity, methodically displayed.

ibid.

This is a common trait of the English character, deficiency in expansion and amiability.

H. Taine, *Notes sur l'Angleterre*, 1871

From the Teutonic womb proceed its slowness, its patience, its coolness, its headstrong courage. This origin will explain the submissiveness of so many unemotional dull commonplace lives, lives that never soar above the dust and are void of hope, will explain this self-tormenting rage not for what is perfect but for what is better . . ., this religion that calls for reasons and is dissatisfied with the past while remaining a slave to its forms.

> A. Laugel, *L'Angleterre politique et social*, 1873
> (transl. J. M. Hart, 1874)

That comfortable people, sitting contentedly on their firm anchored isle, are under no pressing necessity of comparing themselves with anybody. The English, certainly, have this advantage, if it be an advantage. The longitude of character and custom is reckoned from Greenwich.

> E. S. Nadal, *Impressions of London Social Life*, 1875

The lack of breeding, so often noticeable among the English, even of the upper classes.

> Bismarck, 10.xi.1879

John Bull, upon his death-bed, invariably says to his heir: My son, get money, honestly if you can; but get money.

> Max O'Rell [Paul Blouet], *John Bull*
> *and His Island*, 1883

A nation of ants, morose, frigid, and still preserving the same dread of happiness and joy as in the days of John Knox.

> *ibid.*

This species of hypocrisy, entirely English, which they call 'cant' — was substituted for the show of vice . . . for 'cant', the Prince Albert's own creation, is only the quintessence of the national 'Tartufferie'.

> P. Daryl, *La Vie Publique en Angleterre*, 1884
> (transl. H. Frith, 1884)

The temperament of the English, at once violent and sanguine, imposes on them both rigidity in virtue and unrestrainedness in vice.

> J. P. Oliveira Martins, *A Inglaterra de hoje*, 1892
> (transl. C. J. Willdey, 1896)

The people have no mirth. They groan instead of sing; they mutter instead of speak. They move about heavily and in silence.

ibid.

From drink to drunkenness is an easy transition, especially in a climate like that of Great Britain. . . . The drunkenness that debases, brutalises, and maddens, seems to be peculiar to the British soil.

Bahrāmjī M. Malabāri, *The Indian Eye
on English Life*, 1893

Here in England the aggrieved seems to thirst for blood, you smell blood in his protests, in his familiar conversation, there is blood even in his jokes when John Bull is in a jocular mood. Who can say how much of the blood-thirstiness and blood-guiltiness of the people is due to this love of blood or how much of the latter is due to his innate supply of bad blood?

ibid.

The English are, physically and morally, a powerful race, but are intellectually heavy and sluggish. Witty Englishmen are so rare that if one meets a lively Englishman one might rightly suspect that he has Celtic or Continental blood in his veins.

G. F. Steffen, *Från det moderna England*, 1894

. . . attitude of insular superiority and contempt for everything foreign that makes the British traveller cordially detested everywhere on the face of the earth.

G. B. Adams, *Why Americans dislike England*, 1896

In everything touching his nation the Briton is as arrogant as he is tactless. Hence the well-known comment of the Germans in England, 'An individual Englishman may be a very nice fellow, but as a nation they are an impudent lot.'

A. Tille, *Aus Englands Flegeljahren*, 1901

Every Briton clings with all his tentacles to what is old. To be convinced of something new, he needs first to have his whole world fall about his ears.

ibid.

The British officer is to be encountered in only two species. He is either a gentleman or—the other. The officer of the first species is prepared to be charitable to his antagonists, and generally assumes an attitude of dignity and humanity; whereas the latter possesses all the attributes of the idiot, and is not only detestable in the eyes of his antagonists, but is also despised by his own entourage.

General B. Viljoen, *My Reminiscences of the*
Anglo-Boer War, 1902

'Hesitating, humming and drawling are the three Graces of the English conversation', as a wit once said. No other people exhibits in the same degree the contrast and paradox of genius —and an incomparable poetic sensibility in the chosen few— with an extraordinary dullness and cerebral aridity in the masses.

E. Boutmy, *Essai d'une psychologie politique*
du peuple anglais . . ., 1901

Like their sensibilities, their physical imagination—by that I mean the faculty of visualising sensations—is dull and sluggish.

ibid.

Voluptuousness is here not intermingled with the delicate impressions, light diversions, and pleasures of conversation which should be part of it. The Englishman makes straight for the object of his desires. He goes for it as if there were nothing in the world but himself and the object.

ibid.

The fundamental basis of the English character will remain the same for all time and through each change of government or policy—whether democracy or oligarchy, monarchy or republic, free trade or protective rights. Indeed, in spite of the enormous differences of character that it presents from one century to another, the English people have remained and will remain highly individual, incapable of, and impervious to, sympathy, very proud even in the humility of an intense devotion, contemptuous of other nations and ill-suited to mix with them, incapable of comprehending, even from a distance, the solidarity of the civilised world, inclined to divide up questions and consider them piecemeal, with no thought of combining them in the harmony of a vast synthesis, employing logic rather in framing excuses too late than in discovering new horizons, more inclined to stand by a distinguished states-man in all his vicissitudes than to adhere strictly to principles which might condemn him.

ibid.

Yes, great Master! you judged them aright,
Mammoths as they are in perfidy:
They claim from Heaven their descent
And lisp in *English* when they lie.

Kladderadatsch, England-Album, 1914
(misrepresenting Goethe)[1]

Covetousness, a huckstering spirit, a thirst for gain, calculating envy, hypocrisy—what despicable vices have they not become to us. We spit at them, we hate them, just because they are British, allied to British falsehood and craft. We certainly must confess to our shame that *we* also had our share of them; but now we have thrust them all from us, now we walk in gentle innocence through homely pastures, free from greed of money, stripped of all cunning because—just because it is all British.

Pastor Dietrich Vorwerk, *Vaterländische
evangelische Kriegsvorträge,* 1915 (*see* W. W. Coole
and M. F. Potter, *Thus Spake Germany,* 1941)[2]

Brutal lack of consideration, base egoism, selfish behaviour,

---

[1] Goethe wrote (*Faust*): 'Und lispeln englisch, wenn sie lügen' ('englisch' meaning 'like angels').
[2] Cited in future references as 'Coole and Potter'.

when it is to his own advantage: this was always England's way.

Vice-Admiral Kirchhoff, *Englands Willkür und bisherige Allmacht zur See*, 1915

The conceit and unparalleled arrogance of the Englishman leaves nothing to be desired.

ibid.

A people as uncouth and besotted as the British cannot possibly have a high moral standard. And indeed, in pharisaically pious Albion, whose prudery is a household word, we find the utmost moral turpitude.

S. Gopčević, *Das Land der unbegrenzten Heuchelei* (Land of unlimited hypocrisy), 1915

Treason, hypocrisy, lying, envy, cowardice and vileness are the titles of honour of this British nation that imagines it has a monopoly of humanity.

F. Brüggemann, *Die Einheit Europas*, 1915 (*see* Coole and Potter)

The English need an astonishing amount of sleep. It is quite amazing, the capacity they have for sinking into a kind of mental sleep with their eyes still open. One is always meeting those fortunate men who are able to sit by the fire for hours, day after day, without doing or saying anything; at most they smoke one pipe after another. . . . It is only in England that clubs, where members meet to sit in silence and read their newspapers, are one of the necessities of life.

M. Frischeisen-Köhler, 'Das englische Volk und die Kultur', *Das englische Gesicht*, 1915

The defect that most struck an American was its enormous waste in eccentricity. Americans needed and used their whole energy; but English society was eccentric by law and for sake of the eccentricity itself.

The commonest phrase overheard at an English club or dinnertable was that So-and-So 'is quite mad'. It was no offence to So-and-So; it hardly distinguished him from his fellows; and when applied to a public man, like Gladstone, it was qualified by epithets much more forcible. Eccentricity was so general as to become hereditary distinction. It made the chief charm of English society as well as its chief terror.

Henry Adams, *The Education of Henry Adams*,
1918 (pr. printed 1907)

When they are very miserable, they smile. When they are very happy, they say nothing at all. And *au fond* John Bull is terribly sentimental, which explains everything.

A. Maurois, *Les Silences du Colonel Bramble*, 1918
(trans. Thurfrida Wake, 1919)

'I have never seen', said the padre, 'any creatures so stupid, so wicked, so rotten or so dense as English doctors.'

ibid.

He travels through the world with one eye shut, hops all over it on one leg and plays all his scales with one finger.

G. Santayana, *Soliloquies in England*, 1922

The appeal to 'the character of the English people' compels us to recall that this character was welded by the hammer of the civil war between Cavaliers and Roundheads. The character of the Independents; of the petty bourgeoisie, traders, artisans, free landowners, the small local landlord nobility—of the practical, the religious, the economical, the industrious, the enterprising class—clashed inimically with the character of the slothful, dissolute, and arrogant governing classes of old England, the court nobility, titled bureaucracy, and episcopacy.

L. Trotsky, *Where is Britain going?*, 1926

True to his inveterate insularity, our Englishman remains entirely self-satisfied. His century-old pride prevents him from seeing, or at least appreciating, what is wrong with him, especially when he is enumerating his own short-comings, for self-criticism is a very English affectation.

A. Siegfried, *La Crise britannique* . . .
(trans. H. A. and D. Hemming), 1931

The Englishman not only shrinks from the effort to solve his problems; he will not even formulate them. His mental laziness is extraordinary.

ibid.

Shylock's words 'fed with the same food, hurt with the same weapons, subject to the same diseases, healed by the same means, warmed and cooled by the same winter and summer' may apply to Jew and Gentile under other skies, but I shall always be most cautious before I extend it to the Englishman.

G. J. Renier, *The English: Are they Human?*, 1931

The attractive wistfulness of so many Englishmen is in all probability due to repression. It is the manifestation of suffering which has not become acutely unbearable. Nonsense-poetry like that of Lear and of Lewis Carroll could not have been written with such beautiful perfection by a nation that possessed a complete psychological balance.

ibid.

The nation loves its executioners, and experiences a thrill of self-righteous satisfaction at the news of each artificial extinction of life.

ibid.

The normal human being responds to every stimulus from outside: he is essentially and thoroughly alive. And his response is always perceptible.

Now it would be impossible to say the same thing of the English. To begin with, their ataraxy, their reserve, their inarticulateness, muffle the sound of their response. But their response itself is different. It is not the natural and logical end of a chain of events. The English always seem to stand at one remove at least from life, and between their perception of its stimulus and their response to it a series of modifications arises which makes the response entirely unexpected and un-recognizable to anyone who is used to the psychology of the more normal human being.

ibid.

The English compromise in every domain, as naturally, inevitably, and unconsciously as the human lungs breathe air.
. . . Because compromise is his fundamental cerebral process, the Englishman will not make up his mind at once on any question. He funks it. He'll patch it up, he'll snip bits out of it and stick bits on to it; he'll darn it and repair it and freshen it up; but he won't thresh it out, uproot it, and start again without it.

Odette Keun, *I discover the English*, 1934

Dear, likeable, self-fooling, preposterous John Bull! Whoever advised him to choose the lion as his national emblem? He should have been offered an ostrich with its head in the sand.

ibid.

Whether it is the peculiar mixture of oxygen and nitrogen that makes the English mentality, or the strong English mentality that paralyses the natural function of the air, I do not know; all I know is that the air is apathetic and so are the English— even in love.

C. Hansen, *The English Smile*, 1935

Different countries have adopted different animals as symbols of their ambition or character —the eagle of the United States of America and of Germany, the lion and bull-dog of England, the fighting-cock of France, the bear of old Russia. Most of them are aggressive, fighting animals, beasts of prey. It is not surprising that the people who grow up with these examples before them should mould themselves consciously after them and strike up aggressive attitudes, and roar, and prey on others.

J. Nehru, *An Autobiography*, 1936

In the nineteenth century the British ruling classes were the aristocrats of the world, with a long record of wealth and success and power behind them. This long record and training gave them some of the virtues as well as failings of aristocracy. . . . They began to think themselves —as so many races and nations have done —the chosen of God and their empire as an earthly Kingdom of Heaven. If their special position was acknowledged and their superiority not challenged, they were gracious and obliging, provided that this did them no harm. But opposition to them became opposition to the divine order, and as such was a deadly sin which must be suppressed.

ibid.

The British are an insular race and long success and prosperity has made them look down on almost all others. For them, as someone has said, 'les nègres commencent à Calais'.

ibid.

Next to unpunctuality, the most dangerous vice of the English . . . is the morbid abuse of letter-writing.

A. Maurois, *Three Letters on the English*, 1938

There is no nation which stands criticism, even severe criticism, so well as the English. They are too proud to be touchy.

ibid.

I admire profoundly the English sense of leisure and indifference to the passing of time, but one can hardly help seeing that the reason the English have more time is because they do things less thoroughly. They always stop before they have finished the job.

A good many jobs, I suppose, stand in no essential need of finishing. It is not a law of nature that shoes should be shiny or that, providing it works properly, a toilet should refrain from looking as though it had been whittled out of the village stocks. And yet it seems to me the English pay dearly for their repose in slovenliness, discomfort and incuriosity. My fantastic countrymen work themselves into tatters trying to establish havens of hundred-per-centness in a universe geared to incompletion. The English, taking the opposite tack, eschew the temptations of achievement and symmetry and lie quietly down to let the universe roll over them. It frees the juices, I am bound to admit, but it leaves the poor Britons considerably mashed.

M. Halsey, *With Malice toward Some*, 1938

What makes an American realise sinkingly that this, by God, is alien corn is the relative scarcity of laughter. You can get a kind of whinnying sound out of the well-bred English merely by saying that it is raining, and the English who are not well-bred have a superlative gift for catching the humour of a situation. But when it comes to humorous language, American similes and metaphors land with a morbid thump in the midst of a morbid silence. The only way to make the English laugh, as laughter is understood in the United States, is to jab them with your elbow and say out of the corner of your mouth, 'That's funny'. Then they all look nervously around at each other and allow you two decibels of politely acquiescent mirth.

ibid.

ENGLAND EXPECTS

Let us pause to consider the English.
Who when they pause to consider themselves they get all
    reticently thrilled and tinglish,
Because every Englishman is convinced of one thing, viz.:
That to be an Englishman is to belong to the most exclusive
    club there is;
A club to which benighted bounders of Frenchmen and
    Germans and Italians et cetera cannot even aspire to belong,
Because they don't even speak English, and the Americans are
    worst of all because they speak it wrong.
Englishmen are distinguished by their traditions and cere-
    monials,
And also by their affection for their Colonies and their con-
    tempt for their Colonials.
When foreigners ponder world affairs, why sometimes by
    doubt they are smitten,
But Englishmen know instinctively that what the world needs
    most is whatever is best for Great Britain.
They have a splendid Navy and they conscientiously admire it,
And every English schoolboy knows that John Paul Jones was
    only an unfair American pirate.
English people disclaim sparkle and verve,
But speak without reservations of their Anglo-Saxon reserve.

After listening to little groups of English ladies and gentlemen
at cocktail parties and in hotels and Pullmans, of defining
Anglo-Saxon reserve I despair,
But I think it consists of assuming that nobody else is there.
And I shudder to think where Anglo-Saxon reserve ends when
I consider where it begins,
Which is in a few high-pitched statements of what one's
income is and what foods give one a rash and whether one
and one's husband sleep in a double bed or twins.
All good young Englishmen go to Oxford or Cambridge and
they all write and publish books before their graduation,
And I often wondered how they did it until I realised that they
have to do it because their genteel accents are so developed
that they can no longer understand each other's spoken
words so the written word is their only means of inter-
communication.
England is the last home of the aristocracy, and the art of
protecting the aristocracy from the encroachments of
commerce has been raised to quite an art,
Because in America a rich butter-and-egg man is only a rich
butter-and-egg man or at most an honorary LL.D. of some
hungry university, but in England why before he knows it
he is Sir Benjamin Buttery, Bart.
Anyhow, I think the English people are sweet,
And we might as well get used to them because when they slip
and fall they always land on their own or somebody else's
feet.

Ogden Nash, The Face is Familiar, 1940

I like to listen to the Germans talking English on the radio.
There was a very funny one the other day.

He said he was very much in earnest, he said that the English
were a terrible people and he gave two examples of their
passion for unusual cruelty.

In the first place there was the horrible fact that they killed
unborn children, they believe and they preach that most
horrible of doctrines, birth control, can, said he, such a nation
remain in the ranks of the nations called human, no he thought
not, and then he went on there is something almost more

frightful there is Malthus one of their great men who says people should be killed off by plagues, by famine, and by wars, can went on the radio speaker can a country whose acknowledged great men preach such a doctrine, can they be called human.

Gertrude Stein, *Wars I have Seen*, 1945

In ways and means the English are extremely conservative; they dislike reversions and violent revulsions; they rarely ever destroy an institution. They put a skyscraper next to a thatched cottage without being worried by the blatant incongruity. Their approach to life is organic, not mechanic. Yet all the time British affairs are in a flux.

M. J. Bonn, *Wandering Scholar*, 1949

There are, however, many Englishmen—and they are by far the more numerous—for whom sensuality—be it culinary, amatory or artistic—means nothing at all. Nearly the whole people and a good part of the middle class. As for the people, their blindness toward every kind of sensuality is, so to speak, innocent. They do not even realise the existence of the world of enjoyment. They eat anything, even shepherd's pie or steak and kidney pudding or some kind of sticking-paste no bill-poster would look at, which for some unknown reason, they describe as *porridge*, though it has nothing to do with the well-known Scotch delicacy; they drink black Indian tea, a truly infernal drink; and they reproduce themselves by a form of spontaneous generation not yet fully known to biologists. There is no lack of these 'innocent' insensibles in the middle-class; but here one also comes across types more conscious of their own indifference towards the things of the mind, and even proud of it. One of them, related to an illustrious house, once said to me: 'I cannot tell a Picasso from a Raphael.' He was bragging.

S. de Madariaga, *Portrait of Europe*, 1952

At last you English are achieving the impossible—you are making us lose our national sense of humour. For years, insults and sneers have been wafted across the ocean at us and we even imported lecturers who told us in clipped, forceful speech that we were braggarts, uneducated, money-mad, homicidal, crude. Then a lot of us began to travel in England. ... We met a man who kept £10,000 in his safe and counted it for us, not once but three times. We read about whole families being poisoned and attended the trial of a murderer who made Jack the Ripper sound mild. A woman expectorated out of the window of a crowded bus, and we thought longingly of the $50 fine she would have received in America. We had tepid baths in cracked bath-tubs, almost swallowed pits that loitered in plum puddings, choked over watery brussels sprouts, and watched butchers chasing flies from meat left exposed to the elements. We attended vaudeville shows which for sheer vulgarity could not be matched in any country. ... We spent one unforgettable day at Blackpool and decided that our counterpart, Coney Island, is a model town of chivalry and refinement.

> Stella Dean, letter in *The Times*, Sept. 1953

If it were not for his four-footed friends, many an Englishman would burst with suppressed emotion.

> Emily Hahn, *Meet the British*, 1953

Paralytic sycophants, effete betrayers of humanity, carrion-eating servile imitators, arch-cowards and collaborators, gang of women-murderers, degenerate rabble, parasitic traditionalists, play-boy soldiers, conceited dandies.

> Approved terms of abuse for the use of East German Communist speakers when describing Britain, quoted in *The Sunday Times*, 30.viii.1953

In Mexico we think of the Englishman as cold, distant and monocled.

> Carmen Prietto (recorded in the *Star*, 23.xi.1954)

John Bully, John Bully!

> Shouted by Moscow crowds outside British Embassy during Suez crisis, 1956

The defect of many English people is that they cart England around with them to the point of insanity.

M. Guy Mollet (recorded in *The Sunday Times*, 2.ii.1958)

Culture

Wie eng, wie englisch!
Heine, 1838

The English language is broken German mixed with French and British terms, and words, and pronunciation, from which they have also gained a lighter pronunciation, not speaking out of the heart as the Germans, but only prattling with the tongue.

> E. van Meteren, *Nederlandtsche Historie*, 1599
> (*see* W. B. Rye, *England as seen by Foreigners*, 1865)

Every man of taste . . . will find but little Pleasure in reading the *English* Comedies, which are oftener stuff'd with Rants of Wit and Obsceneness, than with fine passages.

> L. de Muralt, *Lettres sur les Anglois*, 1725
> (transl. 1726)

The English have borrowed, disguised and ruined most of Molière's plays.

> Voltaire, *Dictionnaire Philosophique*, 1732

The same causes which deprive the English of any genius for painting or music, deny them equally a gift for tragedy.

> Voltaire, Preface to *Mérope*, 1744

The English plays are like English puddings; nobody has any taste for them but themselves.

> Voltaire, recorded in Spence, *Anecdotes*, 1820

I am certainly very far from being able to approve of *Hamlet* as a tragedy; it is a gross and barbarous play, which would not be tolerated by the lowest audiences in France or Italy. Hamlet goes mad in Act II, and his mistress in Act III; the prince murders his mistress's father while pretending to kill a rat, and the heroine throws herself into the river. Her grave is dug on the stage; the gravediggers make the usual low punning remarks, holding the while the skulls of the dead in their hands; Prince Hamlet replies to their coarse utterances with crazy remarks no less disgusting. While this is happening, one of the actors goes off and conquers Poland. Hamlet, his mother and his step-father drink together on the stage; at the festive board there is singing, fighting and murder; this play might almost be the product of the imagination of a drunken savage. But amongst these coarse irregularities, which, even today, make the English stage absurd and barbarous, one finds in *Hamlet*, by an even greater contrast, sublime traits worthy of the greatest genius.

> Voltaire, Preface to *Sémiramis*, 1749

Your nation two hundred years since is used to a wild scene, to a crowd of tumultuous events, to an emphatical poetry mixed with loose and comical expressions, to murders, to a lively representation of bloody deeds, to a kind of horror which seems often barbarous and childish, all faults which never stained the Greek, the Roman or the French stage; and give me leave to say that the politest of your countrymen differs not much in point of tragedy from the taste of a mob at a bear-garden. 'Tis true we have too much of words, if you have too much of action, and perhaps the perfection of the art should consist in a due mixture of the French taste and the English energy. Mr Addison, who would have reached to that pitch of perfection had he succeeded in the amorous part of his tragedy as well as in the part of Cato, warned often your nation against the corrupted state of the stage—and since he could not reform the genius of the country, I am afraid the contagious distemper is past curing.

> Voltaire, Letter in English to Lord Lyttleton,
> 11.V.1750

The manner of teaching, in the two English universities, what is called in the schools philosophy, is, as I shall show afterwards, rather unphilosophical. But such old Gothic and scholastic institutions are not the rules by which the state of philosophy in England is to be judged.

> G. E. A. Wendeborn, *A View of England*, 1791

I have read Shakespeare and there is nothing in him which approaches Corneille or Racine.

> Napoleon to Thibaudeau, 1803 (quoted in
> J. H. Rose, *The Life of Napoleon I*, 1934)

And what makes the English poets so misanthropic, and diffuses over their writings the unpleasant feeling of antipathy towards everything, is that, with the manifold complications of their obligations to the State they have to devote, if not their whole life, at least the greater part of it, to one party or another.

> Goethe, *Dichtung und Wahrheit*, 1814

English plays,
Atrocious in content,
Absurd in form,
Objectionable in action,
Execrable English theatre!

> Goethe, undated

May it not be that the long separation of the English nation from the classical parts of Europe has gradually altered its taste in the arts? that its pottery, its furniture, its candelabras no longer show purity, lightness and elegance of form? that they have fallen into this contorted, Gothic style, in these heavy, complicated ornaments which represent nothing at all? that the designs of the materials and their choice of colours lag behind the rest of Europe and that England cannot get back into the swim without a long and active association with the Continent?

> Jean-Baptiste Say, *De L'Angleterre et des Anglais*, 1815

And so it only needed a Newton to foist the grotesque theory of light refraction on the human mind, and blind the most cautious investigators to all progressive discoveries.

> Goethe to Esenbeck, August 1816

British women dance as though they were riding on donkeys.

> Heine, *Gedanken und Einfälle*, 1826–47

The devil take these people and their language! They take a dozen monosyllabic words in their jaws, chew them, crunch them and spit them out again, and call that speaking. Fortunately they are by nature fairly silent, and although they gaze at us open-mouthed, they spare us long conversations.

> Heine, *Florentinische Nächte*, 1837

The worst features of the English press are connected with the mystifications, false principles, falsehoods, calumnies, national and personal, and flagrant contradictions that are uttered precisely with a view to conciliate the varying and vacillating interests that depend on the fluctuations and hazards of trade, the public funds, and all those floating concerns of life, which, being by their very nature more liable to vicissitudes than homely industry, most completely demonstrate the truth of the profound aphorism which teaches us that 'the love of money is the root of all evil'.

> J. Fenimore Cooper, *England*, 1837

I feel sick at heart when I reflect that Shakespeare was, after all, an Englishman, and belongs to the most loathsome race that God ever created in His anger.

What a repulsive nation, what a disagreeable country! How strait-laced, how commonplace, how egotistical, *wie eng, wie englisch!*[1]

> Heine, *Shakespeares Mädchen und Frauen*, 1838

[1] As a pun on *eng* (narrow) it cannot be translated.

They, the sons of Albion, are the world's worst dancers, and Strauss declares that there is not one of them that can keep in step. And when in the county of Middlesex, he nearly died when he saw Old English dancing. These people have no ear, either for rhythm or music, and their unnatural passion for pianoforte playing and singing is thus all the more repulsive. There is nothing on earth more terrible than English music, except English painting. They have no sense of sound, or eye for colour, and I sometimes wonder whether their sense of smell is not equally blunted and dulled: I should not be surprised if they cannot even distinguish between the smell of a ball of horse-dung and an orange.

Heine, *Lutezia*, 1840

Ignorance of Kantian philosophy, even after seventy years — a disgrace to Englishmen of learning — is chiefly responsible for this whole wretched isolation of the English.

Schopenhauer, *Die Welt als Wille und Vorstehung*, 2nd ed., 1844

Italian is a language for singing,
German to convey thought,
Greek for representation,
Latin for oratory,
French for causerie,
Spanish for lovers,
and English for coarse brutes.

F. Grillparzer, *Sprachliche Studien*, 1845–6

In England, which has not had its Voltaire, where philosophy is held in slight regard, and thought has less activity than matter, the spirit seems condemned to revolve eternally upon itself, and finds no outlet but by replunging into the past.

A. A. Ledru-Rollin, *De la Décadence de l'Angleterre*, 1850

They are as awkward at a frolic as a bear at a dance.

Horace Greeley, *Glances at Europe*, 1851

One sees in their stolid looks and incurious minds a fatal hopelessness, the natural consequence of a fixed and limited destiny; and taking the press as a chart whereby the degree and quality of national culture may be estimated, do we not daily find in the ferocious personalities and ungenerous comments on other governments, and in the revolting details of crime, painful traces of barbaric tastes? From the iron rule of a mercantile company in London over millions of Hindus, on the other side of the globe, to the savage delight exhibited by the mob in the bloody scenes of the ring, there is evident a gross love of brute force inconsistent with high civilisation.

Henry Tuckerman, *A Month in England*, 1853

Everyone who lives here is so convinced of the contemptibleness, insolence, corruption and baseness of the English press, that I do not like even to soil my hands with touching one of these papers.

Richard Wagner, letter from London, 1855

The orchestra, which has taken a great liking to me, is very efficient . . . but it is quite spoilt as regards expression; there is no *piano*, no *nuance*. With two further rehearsals I hope to put it tolerably in order. But then this hope and my relations with the orchestra are all that I find attractive here: for the rest, everything alienates and disgusts me.

Richard Wagner, letter from London to Liszt,
March 1855

It is strange that England alone has not inherited from her children: Shakespeare and Scott have had no pupils; Milton died in obscurity; the genius of Hogarth remained sterile, and the exiled glory of Byron was not even great enough to get him a grave in his own country.

F. Wey, *Les Anglais chez Eux*, 1856

A good Englishman shuts himself out of three fourths of his mind, and confines himself to one fourth.

R. W. Emerson, *English Traits*, 1856

The English mind turns every abstraction it can receive into a portable utensil, or working institution.

ibid.

Nothing comes to the bookshops but politics, travels, statistics, tabulation and engineering, and even what is called philosophy and letters is mechanical in its structure, as if inspiration had ceased, as if no vast hope, no religion, no song of joy, no wisdom, no analogy, existed any more. The tone of colleges, and of scholars and of literary society has this mortal air. I seem to walk on a marble floor where nothing will grow. They exert every variety of talent on a lower ground, and may be said to live and act in a sub-mind. They have lost all commanding views in literature, philosophy and science.

ibid.

[re *The Times*] Was never such arrogancy as the tone of this paper. Every slip of an Oxonian or Cantabrigian who writes his first leader, assumes that we subdued the earth before we sat down to write this particular *Times*. One would think the world was on its knees to *The Times* office, for its daily breakfast. But this arrogance is calculated. Who would care for it, if it 'surmised', or 'dared to confess', or 'ventured to predict', etc. No; *it is so,* and so it shall be.

ibid.

There is cramp limitation in their habit of thought, sleepy routine, and a tortoise's instinct to hold hard to the ground with his claws, lest he should be thrown on his back. There is a drag of inertia which resists reform in every shape;—law-reform, army-reform, extension of suffrage, Jewish franchise, Catholic emancipation—the abolition of slavery, of impressment, penal code, and entails.

ibid.

The Englishman speaks with all his body. His elocution is stomachic.

ibid.

The English comedy-writers depict these vices, and possess

them. Their talent and their drama are tainted with them. Art and philosophy are absent. The authors do not proceed to a central theme, nor by the most direct route. Their composition is bad, and they are embarrassed by a wealth of material. Their dramas usually contain two intermingled plots, quite independent of each other, and only combined to multiply the incidents, and because the public demands an excess of characters and action. They need a strong current of boisterous action to stir up their sluggish senses; they do as the Romans did, who compressed several Greek plays into one. They are bored with the French simplicity of action, because they lack the refined taste of the French. . . . When a scene begins to develop, a deluge of happenings interrupts it. Superfluous dialogue is spun out between the incidents, like a book where the notes are inserted at random in the middle of the text. There is no carefully thought-out plan; they just took a skeleton plot, as it were, and wrote out the scenes one after another, just as they came. They troubled little about probability; there are poorly affected disguises, ill-feigned madnesses, grotesque marriages, and attacks by robbers worthy of the comic opera.

H. Taine, Hist. de la Litt. Angl., 1863

The interior of an English head may not unaptly be likened to one of Murray's 'Handbooks', which contain many facts and few ideas; a quantity of useful and precise information, short statistical abridgments, numerous figures, correct and detailed maps, brief and dry historical notices, moral and profitable counsels in the guise of a preface, no view of the subject as a whole, none of the literary graces, a simple collection of well-authenticated documents, a convenient memorandum for personal guidance during a journey.

H. Taine, Notes sur l'Angleterre, 1871
(transl. 1872)

Everything that can be done with money, good sense and patience, they do, but of the arts they have no more idea than my cat.

Prosper Mérimée, Lettres à une Inconnue, 1874
(letter of 1850)

I passed yesterday in the new House of Commons, which is a frightful monstrosity; before this I had no idea of what could be accomplished with an utter want of taste and two millions sterling.

ibid.

I am worn out with the perpendicular architecture, and the manners, equally perpendicular, of the natives.

ibid.

They are not a philosophical race—these English: Bacon represents an *attack* on the philosophical spirit in general, Hobbes, Hume and Locke a lowering and debasement of the idea of a 'philosopher' for more than a century.

F. Nietzsche, *Jenseits von Gut und Böse*, 1886

There are truths which are best understood by mediocre minds, there are truths which can charm and seduce only mediocre spirits —one is forced to this possibly unpleasant conclusion at this time when the influence of worthy but mediocre Englishmen—such as Darwin, John Stuart Mill and Herbert Spencer—begins to dominate European middleclass taste. . . . The gulf between knowledge and ability is perhaps greater and more mysterious than one thinks: the able man in the grand style, the creator, may perforce be an ignorant person;—while on the other hand, for scientific discoveries like those of Darwin, a certain narrowness, aridity and careful application (in short something English) may not be a disadvantage.— Finally, let us not forget that the English, with their profound mediocrity, have already brought about once before a general vulgarisation of the European mind. What are called 'modern ideas', or 'the ideas of the eighteenth century' or 'French ideas' against which the *German* mind as a result reacted with profound disgust—are, without any doubt at all, of English origin. The French were only the imitators and exponents of these ideas, their best defenders and at the same time their first and worst victims: for as a result of the diabolical Anglomania of 'modern ideas' the *âme français* has become so thin and emaciated, that at present one recalls its sixteenth and seventeenth centuries, its great passionate strength, its inventive genius, with something approaching incredulity. One must, however, insist on the truth of the verdict of history and defend it against passing prejudice and fashion: the European *noblesse*—of sentiment, taste and manners, in the best sense of the word,—is the work and invention of France; European mediocrity, the plebeianism of modern ideas—is English.

ibid.

Because they have no sun, the English can be neither philosophers nor artists: they have no spark of synthetic genius.

J. P. Oliveira Martins, *A Ingleterra de Hoje*, 1892
(transl. C. J. Willdey, 1896)

The Englishman accepts a fit of delirium if it appears with footnotes, and is conquered by an absurdity if it is accompanied by diagrams.

M. S. Nordau, *Entartung*, 1892, 1893
(transl. 1895)

The taste for philosophy is extremely rare and limited among the English.

E. Boutmy, *Essai d'une psychologie politique du peuple anglais* . . ., 1901

[The Press] These numerous and rapid vehicles of opinion . . . have been used to convey the most blind, selfish and unscrupulous of passions, viz. the thirst for preeminence, contempt for justice, tendency to dispense with traditional forms and to judge of the strength of a country by the violence of its language, determination never to be put in the wrong, and an over-simplified logic incompatible with the rich variety of a complex reality. The Press has become an aid to barbarity.

ibid.

The English are not only unmusical, but decidedly anti-musical.
                         Carl Peters, *England und die Engländer*, 1904
                                                    (transl. 1904)

I believe that Shakespeare cannot be recognized either as a great genius, or even as an average writer.
                                   Leon Tolstoi, *On Shakespeare*
                                     (transl. V. Tchertkoff, 1904)

All his characters speak, not their own, but always one and the same Shakespearean pretentious and unnatural language, in which not only could they not speak, but in which no living man ever has spoken or does speak.

ibid.

Nothing demonstrates so clearly the complete absence of aesthetic feeling in Shakespeare as comparison between him and Homer.

ibid.

The fundamental inner cause of Shakespeare's fame was and is this—that his dramas were 'pro captu lectoris', i.e. they correspond to the irreligious and immoral frame of mind of the upper classes of his time and ours.

ibid.

The suggestion that Shakespeare's works are great works of genius, presenting the height of both aesthetic and ethical perfection, has caused and is causing great injury to men.

This injury is twofold: first, the fall of the drama, and the replacement of this important weapon of progress by an empty and immoral amusement; and secondly, the direct depravation of men by presenting to them false models for imitation.

ibid.

What single cultural work has emerged from the great shop, England, since Shakespeare—except that political abortion, the English state?
                         Werner Sombart, 1914 (*see* Coole and Potter,
                                                    1941)

The English press, the most mendacious and dangerous on God's earth.

'Germanicus', *Das Gift der Presse im Weltkriege*,
1915

Whoever becomes more closely acquainted with England and the English realises very quickly that they have a totally different attitude from ours to spiritual things. The Briton sees the world with other eyes, and art, science, philosophy and religion have a different meaning for him.

M. Frischeisen-Köhler, *Das englische Volk und die Kultur*, 1915 (*see Das englische Gesicht*, 1915)

And then there is, too, the appalling ignorance which strikes the foreigner so forcibly when confronted by the reading matter of the masses, those magazines with their trashy pictures and their even more trashy stories, those newspapers, whose sale depends entirely on the announcement that the prize for a solution of the highly intellectual problem of guessing to a farthing how much money there is in the Bank of England on a given day is a pound a week pension for life, or for supplying the most suitable last line for a limerick a journey to Italy. If one remembers how much sooner England became wealthy than Germany, one is amazed that it is only recently that projects like the *Everymans Library* and the *Home University Library* came into being, lagging generations behind Germany in educational ventures of this kind. It was not the spirit of enterprise that was lacking, but the public, whose abysmal intellectual aridity and disinterestedness, even in the upper classes, is best characterised by the institution of professional entertainers, the 'Society Entertainer'. He is the product of the incapability of society to entertain itself, he is the child of the boredom which lies over England like an atmosphere of lead.

L. L. Schücking, *Der englische Volkscharakter*,
1915

If the French were capable of calm deliberation, they would lynch the owners and editors of *Le Matin* and similar papers, for they are primarily responsible for the terrible fate which has befallen France and given it a death-blow from which it will never recover. And if the British were capable of calm thought they would hang the owners and editors of the *Times* and *Daily Mail*. For the poison press of both countries would not rest until on the one hand France was incited to war, and on the other public opinion in England was so prejudiced against Germany that the British were convinced that Germany must be annihilated, otherwise everything in England would be in jeopardy. (By 'everything' is meant in Britain, of course, merely money.)

> Spiridion Gopčević, *Aus dem Lande der*
> *unbegrenzten Heuchelei*, 1915

The present war has proved that German culture is far superior to present-day British culture.

> W. Franz, *Germanus — Britannien und der Krieg*,
> 1915 (*see* Coole and Potter, 1941)

Of all supposed English tastes, that of art was the most alluring and treacherous. Once drawn into it, one had small chance of escape, for it had no centre or circumference, no beginning, middle, or end, no object, and no conceivable result as education.

> Henry Adams, *The Education of Henry Adams*,
> 1918 (printed 1907)

I think that English humour suffers from the tolerance afforded to the pun. For some reason English people find puns funny. We don't. Here and there, no doubt, a pun may be made that for some exceptional reason becomes a matter of genuine wit. But the great mass of the English puns that disfigure the press every week are mere pointless verbalisms that to the American mind cause nothing but weariness.

But even worse than the use of puns is the peculiar pedantry, not to say priggishness, that haunts the English expression of humour. To make a mistake in a Latin quotation or to stick on a wrong ending to a Latin word is not really an amusing thing. To an ancient Roman, perhaps, it might be. But then we are not ancient Romans; indeed, I imagine that if an ancient

Roman could be resurrected, all the Latin that any of our classical scholars can command would be about equivalent to the French of a cockney waiter on a Channel steamer. Yet one finds even the immortal *Punch* citing recently as a very funny thing a newspaper misquotation of *'urbis et orbis'* instead of *'urbi et orbos'* or the other way round. I forget which. Perhaps there was some further point in it that I didn't see; but, anyway, it wasn't funny.

Stephen Leacock, *My Discovery of England*, 1922

The English writer finds it hard to say a plain thing in a plain way. He is too anxious to show in every sentence what a fine scholar he is. He carries in his mind an accumulated treasure of quotations, allusions, and scraps and tags of history, and into this, like Jack Horner, he must needs 'stick in his thumb and pull out a plum'. Instead of saying, 'It is a fine morning', he prefers to write, 'This is a day of which one might say with the melancholy Jacques, it is a fine morning'.

ibid.

Education counts for so little in England because intelligence itself is not esteemed.

G. J. Renier, *The English: Are they Human?*, 1931

It is a fact recognized by the English themselves that they are bad linguists; in other words, that their intelligence is unable to grasp the subtleties of the grammar of foreign tongues, to penetrate the intricacies of semantic deviations, or divest itself of the fetters imposed on it by childhood and environment.

ibid.

English painting is entirely derivative: it is what study and imitation of the French have made it.

ibid.

Their architecture is the laughing-stock of the Western world.

ibid.

CANT
9 'A terrible war, Reverend!' 'Yes, dreadful — work goes on in the trenches on the Sabbath!' *Simplicissimus*, 1917

ADVICE TO JOHN BULL.

Shut up your Telescope, and don't waste your Tears upon Us. If you want to get up a "Good Cry," look at home.

10 Advice to John Bull, *Vanity Fair* (New York) 1861

Even the ants adapt their building to circumstances. But the English still build as though they lived in the year 1800.

ibid.

Wealthy England has amassed the treasures of the whole world in her collections; none too creative herself, she has carted away the metope of the Acropolis and the Egyptian colossi of porphyry or granite, the Assyrian bas-reliefs, knotty plastic works of ancient Yucatan, smiling Buddhas, Japanese wood-carvings and lacquer-work, the pick of continental art and a medley of souvenirs from the colonies: iron-work, fabrics, glass, vases, snuff-boxes, book-bindings, statues, pictures, enamel, inlaid escritoires, Saracen swords, and heaven alone knows what else; perhaps everything in the world that is of any value.

Karel Čapek, *Letters from England*,
(translated Paul Selver) 1932

Art is what is deposited behind glass in galleries, museums and in the rooms of rich people; but it does not move about here in the streets, it does not twinkle from the handsome cornices of windows, it does not take up its stand at the street-corner like a statue, it does not greet you in a winsome and monu-mental speech. I do not know: perhaps it is only Protestantism which has drained this country dry in an artistic respect.

ibid.

England is the only country on earth that refuses to take the theatre seriously.

C. Hansen (with H. W. Seamen), *The English Smile*, 1935

England has no tragedy of significance, mainly because there is no public demand for it.

ibid.

There is a saying in Hollywood that you don't have to be crazy to get into the movies, but that it helps. In like manner, you do not have to have attended one of Britain's exclusive public schools to become a bishop, a member of the House of Lords, an admiral, a permanent undersecretary for foreign affairs, a governor of the Bank of England, or a prime minister. It simply helps. Now and then a Rufus Isaacs becomes Lord Reading, Viceroy of India, or a Ramsay Macdonald rises to the premiership. But by the time such self-made men have come to the top they are more royalist than the King.

Quincy Howe, *England Expects every American to do his Duty*, 1938

If that fresh deep land had only acted . . . bought, sold, given alms, functioned . . . as she sang in Shakespeare! Danced as a wave o' the sea, instead of turning herself away into the sea's scourge, the world's scourge; robber hypocrite and leech. You see the division that made sweet England ugly? I see it in Shakespeare, the sweet man's false plots, overblown actions.

Waldo Frank, *The Bridegroom Cometh*, 1938

Your acceptance of Shakespeare, your complete satisfaction with Shakespeare, is itself the last word of the dissolution he expressed. You are formless. All you Anglo-Saxon ruling classes. So far you are gone in your dissolution, that you love your chaos, you spread your chaos (ah! England), you make a god and philosophy of your chaos.

ibid.

The English may not always be the best writers in the world, but they are incomparably the best dull writers.

Raymond Chandler, *The Simple Art of Murder*, 1950

Serious discussion gives most Englishmen gooseflesh.

Emily Hahn, *Meet the British*, 1953

Religion

The English are dreadfully given to cant.
Emerson, 1856

Atheism has many followers in England. It may be called the very abyss of blindness, and the uttermost limit of the pestilent heresy of Calvin.

> L. Magalotti, *Travels of Cosmo III, Grand Duke of Tuscany . . .,* 1669 (transl. 1821)

The greater number of the priests are stout and ruddy, and their comfortable appearance convinces you that they lead pleasant and not fatiguing lives. They pass for being rather lazy, and I do not know whether they are maligned, though, to tell the truth, their sermons do not seem to give them much trouble, for they make them very short, and do not lose their time in learning them by heart; they sink their addresses into a velvet cushion and glance at them from time to time, therefore you cannot either truthfully say that they do not learn them at all, and it is only justice to add that you sometimes hear most eloquent preachers whose sermons are touching and convincing, though simple and always short.

> C. de Saussure, *Lettres et Voyages . . . 1725–9,* 1903 (transl. Mme van Muyden, 1902)

Presbyterian ministers never study in universities, and they are generally not only ignorant, but also pedantic, rigid and severe; they scarcely ever smile, they cannot tolerate a jest or joke, and they are so easily scandalised, and altogether so very 'saintly', that you cannot refrain from wondering whether it is entirely sincere. Some of these ministers have been known to write good and useful books, but their number, when compared with their Anglican brethren who have studied deeply at the universities, is very limited.

I think it is principally owing to this sect that Sunday is solemnised as it is in England.

ibid.

They cherish their liberty to such an extent that they often let both their religious opinions and their morals degenerate into licentiousness.

ibid.

England is the country of sectarists. The Englishman, as a free man, prefers to go to Heaven his own way.

Voltaire, *Lettres sur les Anglois*, 1733

Although the clergy of the church of England have good revenues, and though the Bishops live sumptuously, the people do not pay them much respect, and for this reason, the number of religious [*sic!*] and of sects into which the inhabitants are divided, weakens the interest of religion in general, and inspires them with little reverence for the churchmen, who being under no control, live as they please, and not always as they ought. . . . Churchmen are often seen fighting duels. I will not speak of their intoxication, and many other excesses to which they addict themselves without any shame.

J. W. von Archenholz, *England und Italien*, 1785
(transl. 1789, 1791)

Whoever were to judge of the religious character of the English by the frequency with which oaths are administered, and by the carelessness with which they are taken, would certainly think very unfavourably of them.

G. F. A. Wendeborn, *A View of England . . .*,
1791

But they [Methodists and above all Quakers] retain, in their stubborn adherence to their own opinions, in their passionate renunciation of life and in the fanaticism of their faith, the whole physical stamp of the Englishman, which usually manifests itself in stubbornness, selfishness, lack of true wisdom and ignorance of the true value of life.

A. Riem, Reise durch England, 1798–9

There is no Protestant country in Europe, where the ruling party persecutes its dissenting fellow-believers more than in England. There King, government, priests, archbishops, bishops and clergy are unanimous in excluding Britons of different beliefs from all the rights of man.

ibid.

But the English clergy is not without its faults. It neglects too much its duties, is too fond of pleasure, gives too many balls and attends too many public festivities. Nothing shocks a foreigner more than to see a young minister clumsily leading a pretty woman between two lines in an English quadrille.

F. R. Chateaubriand, De l'Angleterre et des Anglais, publ. Mercure de France, 5.vii.1801

If anyone speaks of religion in England, everyone laughs.

Montesquieu, Notes sur l'Angleterre, 1729–32,
publ. 1818

Someone once said, 'Look at this nation: they have dismissed the Father, disowned the Son, and forfeited the Holy Spirit.'

ibid.

. . . the detestable English clergy, with whom stultification of every kind is a thing after their own hearts, so that only they may be able still to hold the English nation, otherwise so intelligent, involved in the most degrading bigotry; therefore, inspired by the basest obscurantism, they oppose with all their might the education of the people, the investigation of nature, nay, the advancement of all human knowledge in general; and both by means of their connections and by means of their scandalous, unwarrantable wealth, which increases the misery of the people, they extend their influence even to university teachers and authors, who accordingly . . . resort to suppressions and perversions of every kind simply in order to avoid opposing even in a distant manner that 'cold superstition' (as Pückler very happily designates their religion, or the current arguments in its favour).

> A. Schopenhauer, *Die Welt als Wille und Vorstehung*, 2nd ed. 1844 (transl. R. B. Haldane, 1883–6)

Lambeth Palace is a monument of ecclesiastical persecution.

> Henry Tuckerman, *A Month in England*, 1853

The English would become Catholics if necessary to get the support of France. They have more cotton wool in their bodies than Protestantism.

> Bismarck to Leopold von Gerlach, 21.xii.1854

England accepted this ornamented national church, and it glazes the eyes, bloats the flesh, gives the voice a stertorous clang, and clouds the understanding of the receivers.

> R. W. Emerson, *English Traits*, 1856

The curates are ill-paid, and the prelates are overpaid. This abuse draws into the church the children of the nobility, and other unfit persons, who have a taste for expense. Thus a bishop is only a surpliced merchant. Through his lawn, I can see the buttons of his shopman's coat glitter. A wealth like that of Durham makes almost a premium upon felony.

> *ibid.*

An Anglican minister, however, would never visit the poor.

> F. Dostoevsky, *Zimnia Zamietki* . . ., 1863

Anglican ministers are haughty and rich, live in wealthy parishes and dioceses and wax fat with an easy conscience. It is a religion of the rich, and blatantly so.

> *ibid.*

The love of money has killed all sense of honour, and all feeling for right and wrong; they disguise their cowardice and sensuality with unctuous theological oratory, which we German heretics find the most repulsive of all the English sins. When we see the English press turning its pious eyes to Heaven over the heathen warriors of the Continent, we are reminded of the whining tones of a parson. As though the all-powerful God, in whose name Cromwell's Ironsides fought, ordered us Germans to let our arch enemy march peacefully into Berlin. O hypocrisy, O cant, cant, cant!

> H. von Treitschke, *Die Feuerprobe Norddeutschen Bundes*, 1870

But what shall it profit a man, if he gain the whole world and lose his own soul? says Scripture. This is just what John Bull thought, and so in the other world he has knocked down to himself the kingdom of Heaven—in his eyes as incontestably a British possession as India or Australia.

> Max O'Rell [Paul Blouet], *John Bull and His Island*, 1883

It is characteristic of such an unphilosophical race to cling firmly to Christianity—they *need* its discipline for 'moralising' and humanising. The Englishman, more gloomy, sensual, stubborn and brutal than the German, is also, as the coarser of the two, more given to piety: he has all the more *need* of Christianity. To finer nostrils, even this English Christianity still has a real English odour of spleen and alcoholic excess, against which it serves as an antidote.

> F. Nietzsche, *Jenseits von Gut und Böse*, 1886

In an English church, more than anywhere else, the thought occurs to the Russian, There are many good things here, yet I am thankful that I was born in Russia. . . . Enter an English church and watch the congregation. It is devout; solemn it may be, but it is a congregation of 'ladies and gentlemen', each with a space specially reserved; the rich in separate and embellished pews, like the boxes of an opera-house. We cannot help thinking that this church is merely a reunion of people in society, and that there is place in it only for what society calls 'the respectable'.

> K. P. Pobyedonostseff, *Reflections . . .*,
> (transl. R. C. Long), 1898

The external Protestantism of England does not attract the German people, not this pious humanitarianism which seeks to conquer gold and empires; but pure Protestantism. A Protestant foundation will protect a justly larger Germany from the hate which is heaped upon pious, self-seeking England.

> H. Wagner, *Die deutsche Weltpolitik*, 1900

The race is religious, for the simple reason that, being by nature violent and brutal, it has a special need of discipline.

> E. Boutmy, *Essai d'une Psychologie du Peuple Anglais*, 1901

John Bull the theologian, instinct with heresy and practising compromise.

> G. Santayana, *Soliloquies in England*, 1922

Parliament and the Union Jack occupy a larger place in the heart of churchmen than the Cross and the Bible.

> G. J. Renier, *The English: Are they Human?*
> 1931

An English Sunday, blighted by unutterable boredom.

> Karel Čapek, *Letters from England* (transl.
> P. Selver), 1932

People go into the country to protect themselves in a wild panic from the English Sunday. On Saturday every Briton is assailed by the blind instinct to escape somewhere, just as an animal flees in a blind instinct from an approaching earthquake. Those unable to flee away, at least seek refuge in church, there to tide over the day of horror in prayers and song. This is the day when nobody cooks, nobody travels, nobody gazes and nobody thinks. I do not know for what unutterable guilt the Lord has condemned England to the weekly punishment of Sunday.

ibid.

To foreign observers it has always seemed one of the least comprehensible and most repulsive sides of the English national character, that in Britain they always have Biblical quotations on their lips and observe strictly the outward form of Christianity whilst their own ethical behaviour towards their fellow men, and especially towards other nations, has always been a sanguinary mockery of the fundamental principles of Christianity.

E. Schulze, *Die Blutspur Englands*, 1940

The classical fiber in British political life was intertwined with a very different strain—Nonconformity. It had none of the graces that the humanists had salvaged from the barbarian invasion, and which may not survive the age of the technocrats. It did not possess the steel-like flexibility of Rome, but it had even greater strength. It drew it from man's close union with his God. Its exalted fanatic individualism bordered almost on anarchism, for the world might perish if true believers could but save their souls. . . . Nonconformity gave a harshness to British liberalism that the humanist rational liberalism of other countries never possessed.

M. J. Bonn, *Wandering Scholar*, 1949

Food

There are in England sixty different
religious sects and only one sauce.
Caracciolo (attrib.)

What does England rear but cattle? Their stomach is their
god, and to the stomach they eagerly pay sacrifice.
Disputatio inter Anglicum et Francum, 1375–7

'French Dog', said an Englishman,
'You do nothing but drink wine.'
'True, we do', said the Frenchman,
'But you drink your pots of beer.'
Eustache Deschamps, late 14th cent.

Go back, you dissolute English,
Drink your beer and eat your pickled beef.
La Répentance des Anglais et des Espagnols, 1522

Flesh-eaters, and insatiable of animal food; sottish and unrestrained in their appetites; full of suspicion.
Nicander Nucius of Corcyra, *Travels*
(transl. J. A. Cramer, 1841), 1545

No beef, no English.
Saint-Amant, *L'Albion*, 1644

The *English* eat a great deal at Dinner; they rest a while, and to it again, till they have quite stuff'd their paunch. Their supper is moderate: Gluttons at Noon, and abstinent at night.

H. Misson de Valbourg, *Mémoires* . . .
(transl. M. Ozell, 1719), 1698

Belching at table, and in all companies whatsoever, is a thing which the *English* no more scruple than they do coughing and sneezing.

ibid.

They all have a tendency to melancholy, especially in the south. Some attribute this to the heaviness of the sea air, and others to the coarseness of the food, particularly too much meat-eating.

G. L. Le Sage, *Remarques sur l'État présent d'Angleterre . . . dans les années 1713 et 1714*, 1715

Though no wines are grown in England, it is no hindrance to drunkenness, for in the day-time the lower classes get intoxicated with liquor and beer, and the higher classes in the evening with Portuguese wines and punch.

C. de Saussure, *Lettres et Voyages . . . 1725-9*,
1903 (transl. Mme van Muyden, 1902)

The English, who eat their meat red and bloody, show the savagery that goes with such food.

J. O. de la Mettrie, *L'Homme Machine*, 1748

All nations of Europe are despised by the sleek, pudding-eating, beer-drinking Englishman.

J. G. Zimmermann, *Vom Nationalstolze*, 1758

Great meat-eaters are generally more cruel and ferocious than other men. English barbarity is well known.

J. J. Rousseau, *Emile*, 1762

The Englishman cooks his soup in his stomach.

G. C. Lichtenberg, *Bruchstücke aus dem Tagebuche von der Reise nach England*, 1775

A thick air, and solid food, make the use of strong liquors necessary in England, and persons that would drink nothing but water there, might soon repent it.

> J. W. von Archenholz, *England und Italien*, 1785 (transl. 1789, 1791)

The tea is always excellent in England, but nowhere do they drink worse coffee.

> B. Faujas de Saint-Fond, *Voyage en Angleterre* . . ., 1797

The nation reputed to be the richest in the world is condemned to slake its thirst with the most dangerous poisons under the name of wine.

> Jean Baptiste Say, *De l'Angleterre et des Anglais*, 1815

Instead of saying, as we do in France, 'to eat one's fill', the English say, 'to eat and drink one's fill'.

> Montesquieu, *Notes sur l'Angleterre*, 1729–32, publ. 1818

May Heaven save every Christian from their sauces, which consist of one-third flour and two-thirds butter, or, for a variation, of two-thirds flour and one-third butter.

> H. Heine, *Florentinische Nächte*, 1837

Poultry is almost tasteless in England . . . and genuine apples are as scarce as rubies.

> [Stephen Fiske] *English Photographs*, by an American, 1869

Their cookery has no savour. I have purposely dined in twenty taverns, from the lowest to the highest, in London and elsewhere. I got large portions of fat meat and vegetables, without sauce; one is amply and wholesomely fed, but one has no pleasure in eating.

> H. Taine, *Notes sur l'Angleterre*, 1871

These islanders, you soon find, have little regard for lightness.

A light dish of eggs in some form, a light roll, fresh butter, coffee and hot milk? Yes, of a sort, but none of them light. You soon forswear coffee for tea, and ere long the passive bulwark of resistance wearies you into eggs and bacon, and cold meat, and jams, for your first meal of the day. Little things are typical. What you want is not refused you, but what they have and like is gradually forced upon you. Thus they govern their colonies. No raising of voices, no useless and prolonged discussion, no heat generated, no ridicule of your habits, or eulogy of their own, none of these, but just slow-moving, unchanging, confident bulk.

Price Collier, England and the English, 1909

Lothrop Motley, who stood among the very best, said to him early in his apprenticeship that the London dinner and the English country house were the perfection of human society. The young man meditated over it, uncertain of its meaning. Motley could not have thought the dinner itself perfect, since there was not then—outside of a few bankers or foreigners— a good cook or a good table in London, and nine out of ten of the dinners that Motley ate came from Gunter's, and all were alike. Every one, especially in young society, complained bitterly that Englishmen did not know a good dinner when they ate it, and could not order one if they were given *carte blanche*.

Henry Adams, The Education of Henry Adams,
1918 (printed 1907)

The English, most emphatically, eat to live.

G. J. Renier, The English: Are they Human?, 1931

English cooking is of two kinds: good and average. Good English cooking is simply French cooking; the average cooking in the average hotel for the average Englishman explains to a large extent the English bleakness and taciturnity. Nobody can beam and warble while chewing pressed beef smeared with diabolical mustard. Nobody can exult aloud while unglueing from his teeth a quivering tapioca pudding.

Karel Čapek, Letters from England, 1932

The truth about the average English cooking can never be stated. There are no adequate words for it. To be believed, it must be eaten. Many things have struck me as prodigious in this country, but none so much as the restraint that the ordinary Englishman practises towards the woman, wife or servant, who prepares his meals. She has first-rate natural produce at her disposal—enormous variety, excellent quality, comparatively low prices. The shops stock for her the finest and cleanest materials in the world. What emerges from her kitchen is diabolical. I've heard some simpletons declare that Puritanism squashed the *joie de vivre* out of the English race. Just glance at the ordinary Englishman's menu, and tell me what *joie de vivre* a man can retain after partaking, on pain of complete starvation, of pressed beef, frizzled fish, watery vegetables, mustard, pink and yellow chemical sauces, gluey and flabby puddings, poisonous and inky tea. It is not to be wondered at that the English eat too little and too hurriedly, that they gulp down, rather than taste, their food, that their devastated palates know not how to distinguish between wines, and that they jump up from table as though their behinds were on fire. The origin of the Englishman's characteristics of taciturnity, solemnity, austerity and general moroseness, is to be found in the Englishwoman's accomplishments. To make a race bleak, there is no need of evoking a vision of eternal torments. Give it the ordinary English meal.

Odette Keun, *I discover the English*, 1934

Today Henry and I and some of the faculty from the college lunched at an Exeter restaurant. It was a bad lunch half cold and wholly watery, and in order to keep body and soul together, I asked for a glass of milk. The waitress was staggered.

'Milk?' she asked incredulously.

'Why, yes,' I replied, almost equally incredulously. 'A glass of milk.'

She wheeled off in the direction of the kitchen. In three minutes she was back again.

'Please', she asked, 'do you want this milk hot or cold?'

I blinked a little and said I wanted it cold. The Englishmen who were with us looked amused. 'You Americans', one of them said, with a spacious tolerance. We resumed our conversation, and in a short space the waitress made a third appearance. She had a hounded expression.

'Do you', she inquired desperately, 'want this milk in a cup or a glass?'

'Just roll it up in a napkin,' I answered thoughtlessly, and then was sorry, seeing how embarrassed and confused she was.[1]

M. Halsey, *With Malice toward Some*, 1938

It's wonderful, it's superb—what a good thing they can't cook it.

Anonymous American passing through
spectacular English scenery, 1954

What one eats in England is not so much food as congeries of synthetic hunger killers.

Gabriel Mouchot, in *Medical World*, 1955

A scientist says: Roast beef made England what she is. Moral: Eat more vegetables.

Anon.

---

[1] This is a puzzling story, seeing that the British public was being positively flooded with milk at this period by a publicity campaign of the Milk Marketing Board.

11 What Mohammed is to the Turk, the Pocketbook is to the
Englishman, from *Simplicissimus*, American edition, 1915

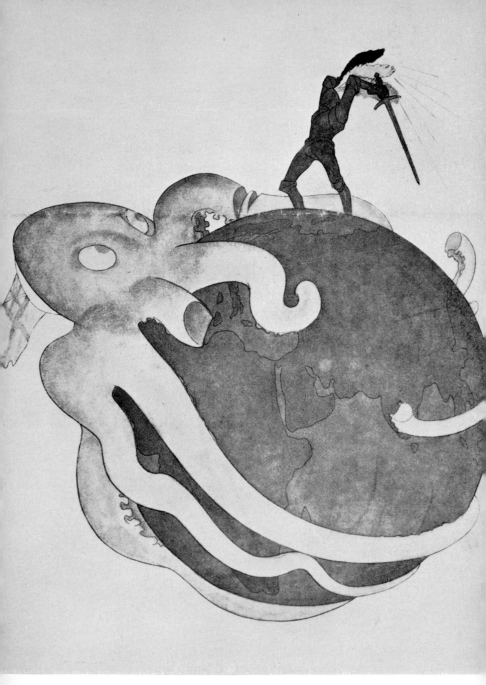

12 Germany Frees the World, *Simplicissimus*, 1917

Economics and Social Life

> The deadly choke-damp of boredom.
> Heine, 1840

About St Paul's there is, as you know, a college of some learned men, who are said to fare well; I reckon it living in a sewer.

> Erasmus to Ammonius, 18.xi.1511

For while these people are nothing but *Cyprian Bulls and dung-eaters* — they think they are the only persons that feed on ambrosia and Jupiter's brain.

> Erasmus to Ammonius, 26.xi.1511

Custom-house officers in this country are extraordinarily clever at discovering anything contraband, a share going into their pockets, and a stranger has often much trouble in recovering his belongings. I had to go to the Customs several times, and wait many days, before I could recover my boxes, and it cost me four or five half-crowns, though I had no sort of contraband goods. It seems to me that making strangers pay for bringing worn clothes into a country is not creditable to the English nation, and I have heard it said that it is the custom in no other country.

> C. de Saussure, *Lettres et Voyages* (transl. as
> *A Foreign View of England* by Mme van Muyden,
> 1902), 1725

Twenty men will sit smoking and reading newspapers in a tavern, they talk so little that you will hear a fly buzz.

ibid.

The English are very fond of a game they call cricket. For this purpose they go into a large open field, and knock about a small ball with a piece of wood. I will not attempt to describe this game to you, it is too complicated; but it requires agility and skill, and everyone plays it, the common people and also men of rank. Sometimes one county plays against another county. The papers give notice of these meetings beforehand, and, later, tell you which side has come off victorious.

ibid.

The *English* Mechanicks have acquired a great deal of Reputation in the World, and in many things not without Reason; ... There are likewise some in which they have got a Name, without any Foundation. Their small pieces of Steel Work are little worth, tho' they set a high Value on them and sell them at a dear Rate; the temper is indeed good, but as for the Workmanship, 'tis ill placed, and ill finished; and generally speaking, they are outdone by the *French* in every kind of Toy Work, which is indeed rather curious than useful, and their best Masters come from *Paris*. The small Experience of the People of this Country in Things of this Kind, must be attributed to their Dislike of Trifles, and their too great Easiness in paying roundly for every thing they buy; the greatest Part of them judge only of a Work by the Price, and you may well think that the Workman, being at no great Pains to please them, and in the way of growing rich at his Ease, is not over diligent in minding his Trade, and consequently will never excel in it.

L. de Muralt, *Lettres sur les Anglois*, 1725
(transl. 1726)

London, the capital where they hawk the most inaccurate news and the worst possible arguments based on complete falsehoods.

Voltaire, *Les Mensonges Imprimés*, 1749

Here are liberty of conscience, political liberty, civil liberty, commercial liberty, liberty of thought, tongue and pen, to and beyond the limits of the most profligate licence; newspapers, magazines, pamphlets, registers; turfs, cockpits, clubs, maccaronies, blackguards, stocks, lotteries, schemes, lame ducks, clever fellows, humour, and Novembers big with suicide; post chaises, Italian music and pictures, but few with eyes or ears; the nest of foreigners; the country of Shakespeare, Newton and Hogarth.

> F. C. von Moser[1] (quoted by S. Collet in
> *Relics of Literature*, 1823) *c*. 1750

The boxing-matches in England, the bull-baiting, the cock-fightings, and the numerous attendance, of both sexes, at public executions, indicate that there is at least a remnant of Roman manners, and of the taste of those times, still left in England.

> G. F. A. Wendeborn, *A View of England . . .*,
> 1791

The municipal laws of England stand, it should seem, more in need of reform than the criminal.

> J. H. Meister, *Souvenirs . . .*, 1791 (transl. 1799)

Let Pitt then boast of this victory[2] to his nation of shopkeepers (*nation boutiquière*).

> Bertrand Barère, Report to the National
> Convention, 16.vi.1794

Hence their great financial system, which reduces 66,000 people to beggary every year. Hence their crass ignorance of religion and philosophy. Hence their unfamiliarity with the history and statistics of other nations. Hence the garrulousness in their modern novels and the spleen of their poets. Hence their conceit, their assumption that they are the noblest nation, because they know no other nations and have no yard-stick of comparison, and because their highest ideal of generosity is measured in guineas and not in human feeling. Hence also their

---

[1] Envoy to Hanover from Elector Palatine.
[2] The Glorious First of June.

insolent behaviour towards foreigners. . . . Hence the barbarity with which they annihilated more people in India than the Spaniards in America. Hence their love of wealth, their lust for riches by any means, and their willingness to sacrifice for bribes the advantages of freedom and become slaves. Hence their savage amusements, the torture of men and animals, and the foolish wagers, which often ruin entire families. Hence their costly pleasures, which have not the grace and pleasing manners of other countries. Hence their tendency to crazy, foolish actions, which in the rest of Europe are called folly, but in England merely *Whim* or *Spleen*, although it is a disease of the mind. . . . Hence, to sum up, their bravery in savage wars at sea and their cowardice in war on land, their contempt for the good of other nations because they know only themselves.

A. Riem, *Reise durch England*, 1798–9

Those wealthy muck-worms, who extorted millions in India, owe their fortunes to trade.

ibid.

It is therefore no wonder that the English, who are fierce lovers of cock-fighting, horse-racing and hunting, also have a great fondness for boxing, in which men batter one another to death.

ibid.

The laws of England are instruments of revenge rather than of justice.

ibid.

I recollect that Paoli, who was a great friend to your nation, in fact who was almost an Englishman, said on hearing the English extolled as the most generous, the most liberal, and the most unprejudiced nation on earth, 'Softly, you go too far; they are not so generous nor so unprejudiced as you imagine; they are very self-interested; they are a nation of merchants, and generally have a gain in view. Whenever they do anything, they always calculate what profit they shall derive from it. They are the most calculating people in existence.' . . . Now I believe that Paoli was right.

> Napoleon, 17.ii.1817 (*see* Barry O'Meara,
> *Napoleon in Exile*, 1822)

You were greatly offended with me for calling you a *nation of shopkeepers*. Had I meant by this that you were a nation of cowards, you would have had reason to be displeased; even though it were ridiculous and contrary to historical facts; but no such thing was ever intended. I meant that you were a nation of merchants, and that all your great riches, and your grand resources arose from commerce, which is true.

> Napoleon, 31.v.1817 (*ibid.*)

An Englishman must have a good dinner, a woman, and comfort; . . . if his business fails him, and he can no longer have them, he either commits suicide or turns thief.

> Montesquieu, *Notes sur l'Angleterre*, 1729–32,
> publ. 1818

How can the English like foreigners when they do not like each other? How can they ask us to dine with them when they do not dine with each other?

> *ibid.*

It has been the peculiar lot of our country to be visited by the worst kind of English travellers. While men of philosophical spirit and cultivated minds have been sent from England to ransack the poles, to penetrate the deserts, and to study the manners and customs of barbarous nations, with which she can have no permanent intercourse or profit or pleasure, it has been left to the broken-down tradesmen, the scheming adventurer, the wandering mechanic, the Manchester and Birmingham agent, to be her oracles respecting America.

> Washington Irving, *The Sketch Book*, 1820

If England is willing to permit the mean jealousies of trade or the rancorous animosities of politics to deprave the integrity of her press and poison the fountain of public opinion, let us beware of her example. She may deem it her interest to diffuse error and engender antipathy for the purpose of checking emigration; we have no purpose of the kind to serve.

ibid.

Ces insulaires marchands.

F. R. Chateaubriand to Villèle, December, 1822

London is now so utterly dead as to elegance and fashion, that one hardly meets an equipage; and nothing remains of the 'beau monde' but a few ambassadors. The huge city is, at the same time, full of fog and dirt, and the macadamized streets are like well-worn roads; the old pavement has been torn up, and replaced by small pieces of granite, the interstices between which are filled with gravel; this renders the riding more easy, and diminishes the noise; but on the other hand changes the town into a sort of quagmire. Were it not for the admirable 'trottoirs', people must go on stilts, as they do in the Landes near Bordeaux. Englishwomen of the lower classes do indeed wear an iron machine of the kind on their large feet.

[H. Fürst von Pückler-Muskau], *Briefe eines Verstorbenen*, 1831 (transl. as *Tour in England . . ., 1826–9*, 1832)

What contributes much to the 'dullness' of English society, is the haughty aversion which Englishmen (note well that I mean in their own country, for 'abroad' they are ready enough to make advances) show to addressing an unknown person; if he should venture to address them, they receive it with the air of an insult . . . .

There is a story that a lady saw a man fall into the water, and earnestly entreated the dandy who accompanied her, and who was a notoriously good swimmer, to save his life. Her friend raised his 'lorgnette' with the phlegm indispensable to a man of fashion, looked earnestly at the drowning man, whose head rose for the last time, and calmly replied, 'It's impossible, Madam, I never was introduced to that gentleman.'

ibid.

Yesterday evening at seven o'clock I left Bath, again by the mail, for Salisbury. My only companion was a widow in deep mourning; notwithstanding which, she had already found a lover, whom we took up outside the town. He entertained us, whenever he spoke of anything but farming, with those horrible occurrences of which the English are so fond that the columns of their newspapers are daily filled with them.

ibid.

Cheating, in every kind of 'sport', is as completely in the common order of things in England, among the highest classes as well as the lowest, as false play was in the time of the Count de Grammont. It is no uncommon thing to hear 'gentlemen' boast of it almost openly; and I never found that those who are regarded as 'the most knowing ones' had suffered in their reputation in consequence;—'au contraire', they pass for cleverer than their neighbours; and you are only now and then warned with a smile to take care what you are about with them.

ibid.

Silence, a conversation with an Englishman.

H. Heine, 1828

Send a philosopher to London, but for Heaven's sake do not send a poet. This unalloyed seriousness in all things, this colossal uniformity, this machine-like motion, this surliness even when joyful, this overdone London, which stifles the imagination and breaks the heart. And if you send a German poet, a dreamer, who would stand and gaze at every single phenomenon, at a ragged beggar-woman or a glittering gold-smith's shop—how badly it will fare with him! He will be pushed by all and sundry or knocked down with a mild 'God damn!' Oh, that accursed shoving! I soon noticed that this nation has much to do. It lives in grand style, and although food and clothing is dearer there than in our own country, it wants to be better clothed and fed than ourselves; and like all nobility, it runs up great debts, but occasionally with ostentation throws a few guineas out of the window, pays other nations to box around for her amusement, and in addition hands its respective kings a substantial pourboire—and so John Bull has to work day and night to amass money for these expenses, rack his brain day and night to invent new machines, and he sits and calculates in the sweat of his brow, and runs and rushes, from the port to the Exchange, from the Exchange to the Strand, and so it is really pardonable if, when he meets a poor German poet on the corner of Cheapside gazing into a shop window and blocking his path, he pushes him aside saying 'God damn!'

H. Heine, *Englische Fragmente*, 1828

Comfort is in the mouth of every Englishman at every moment; it is the half of his life.

Count G. Pecchio, *Osservazioni semi-serie . . .*, 1831 (transl. 1833)

The tavern is the forum of the English.

ibid.

It is only when you see Englishmen in a foreign country that their defects stand out so strongly by force of contrast. They are the very gods of boredom, dashing through one country after another in their black varnished carriages, and leaving a grey cloud of melancholy behind them. And then their curiosity devoid of interest, their 'dolled-up' coarseness, their bold timidity, their angular egoism, and their desolate delight in all melancholy objects.

H. Heine, *Florentinische Nächte*, 1837

Just as machines in England seem like human beings, so are Englishmen like machines. Yes, wood, iron and brass seem to have usurped the spirit of man there and with an excess of spirit gone almost mad, while man, deprived of his soul, acts like a brainless phantom and pursues his daily round in machine-like fashion, at appointed times eating his beef-steak, making parliamentary speeches, brushing his nails, boarding his stage-coach or hanging himself.

ibid.

In England a man dines by himself, in a room filled with other hermits.

> J. Fenimore Cooper, *England* . . ., 1837

That island of damnation, that Botany Bay without a southern climate, that smoke-covered, machine-deafened, churchgoing, badly besotted England.

> H. Heine, *Shakespeares Mädchen und Frauen*, 1838

There is nothing real in the foundation of things in Great Britain except misery, and that is universal. The Government, the public and private banks, the commercial houses of every degree, the agriculturalists and manufacturers—in short, all the characters of the dark drama which has been played so long in England, are struck to the heart, and palsied in their movements. . . . The people, enlightened by the disastrous, yet salutary, example of England, will perhaps comprehend that the science of evil has its limits, and beyond that—there is death.

> A. A. Ledru-Rollin, *De la Décadence de l'Angleterre*, 1850

I have brought manufacturing and mercantile England, which engrossed two-thirds of the commerce of the world, before the assizes of her workmen, and they have answered, 'We die of hunger under her laws, her competitions grind us down, her liberty kills us; it is the robbery of our wages.'

> *ibid.*

When there passed before my eyes . . . deep phalanxes of workmen who trembled with fever under their rags, and who all loudly cursed their country, I understood that England, notwithstanding her apparent grandeur, was on the decline; and it is not my voice, powerless and insignificant in exile, it is her people of the workshops, her people of the fields, her people of the sea, her starving population, which solemnly proclaims her downfall. 'Despair and die', has been the language held out to them by the British aristocracy for ages: 'despair and die', reply the people in their turn.

> *ibid.*

Stultified with beer and tobacco, it is difficult to obtain an intelligent response from any of the lower orders, to the most ordinary question.

H. Tuckerman, *A Month in England*, 1853

England nobly gives an asylum to the life, but not to the soul of the refugee.

ibid.

In this place I feel like a sacrificial lamb. I hope I shall never be in London again.

Richard Wagner, letter from London
to W. Fischer, April 1855

The scenes in Hyde Park last Sunday were disgusting, not only because of the brutality of the police, but because of the lack of resistance of the enormous crowds.

Karl Marx, letter to Engels, July 1855

The nearer we look, the more artificial is their social system. Their law is a network of fictions. Their property, a scrip or certificate of right to interest on money that no man ever saw. Their social classes are made by statute. Their ratios of power and representation are historical and legal. The last Reform-bill took away political power from a mound, a ruin, and a stone-wall, whilst Birmingham and Manchester, whose mills paid for the wars of Europe, had no representative. Purity in the elective parliament is secured by the purchase of seats. Foreign power is kept by armed colonies: power at home by a standing army of police. The pauper lives better than the free labourer; the thief better than the pauper; and the transported felon better than the one under imprisonment. The crimes are factitious, as smuggling, poaching, non-conformity, heresy and treason. Better, they say in England, to kill a man than a hare. The sovereignty of the seas is maintained by the im-pressment of seamen. 'The impressment of seamen', said Lord Eldon, 'is the life of our navy.' Solvency is maintained by means of a national debt, on the principle, 'if you will not lend me money, how can I pay you?' Their system of education is factitious. The universities galvanise dead languages into a semblance of life. Their church is artificial. The manners and customs of society are artificial—made-up men with made-up manners;—and thus the whole is Birminghamised, and we have a nation whose existence is a work of art;—a cold, barren, almost arctic isle, being made the most fruitful, luxurious, and imperial land in the whole earth.

> R. W. Emerson, *English Traits*, 1856

An Englishman who visits Mount Etna, will carry his tea-kettle to the top.

> *ibid.*

High Art in England.
The London correspondent of the *Daily Times* asserts that the upper line of pictures in the Art Gallery of the International Exhibition is situated at the height of thirty feet from the floor. Oil pictures, only, are admitted to that high latitude, as Water would freeze there.

> *Vanity Fair*, (New York) 21.vi.1862

English inns are the dearest, the worst-managed, the most unhome-like in any civilised country.

> [Stephen Fiske] *English Photographs, By an American*, 1869

Women are worse treated in Great Britain than in any other civilised country.

> *ibid.*

The vices of prostitution and adultery underlie all grades of English life, and crop up unmistakably in all phases of English society.

> *ibid.*

An Englishman absolutely believes that he can warm a room by building a grate-fire at the end of it.

> *ibid.*

He has a longing for rough exercise; he has fighting instincts, consequently the desire to conquer, and to earn the proud testimony that he has performed a difficult task. . . . Applying this longing for action and for struggle to trades and to professions, it will produce the requisite energy for supporting their fatigue and yoke, more especially if we take into account two circumstances which greatly lessen the principal weight of modern toil, I mean weariness. The one is the phlegmatic temperament which represses the springs of ideas, the improvisation, the petty intervening emotions, and enables the man to work with the regularity of a machine. The other is the want of nervous delicacy, the acquired insensibility, the being accustomed to dull sensations, which suppress in man the desire for keen and varied pleasure, and hinder him from rebelling against the monotony of his business.

H. Taine, *Notes sur l'Angleterre*, 1871

Dull as a black bug. London. Little sooty-black houses, or big Gothic or Venetian cupboards. Four or five cafés where drink is possible, all the rest are dining-rooms where there is no drink, and coffee houses devoid of all spirits (and *esprit*!). . . . And the theatres! Actors of the time of the late good Noessard, bestial cries, actresses thin enough to make one weep.

P. Verlaine, *À Londres*, 1872

London, black as crows and as noisy as ducks, prudish with all the vices in evidence, everlastingly drunk, in spite of ridiculous laws about drunkenness, immense, though it is really basically only a collection of tiny, scandal-mongering boroughs, vying with each other, ugly and dull, without any monuments except interminable docks.

ibid.

To chat and seek to amuse each other is a thing unknown to the English.

P. Mérimée, *Lettres à une Inconnue*
(letter June 1850), 1874

Lord Beaconsfield could find satisfaction in the fact that he had changed the shopkeeper policy, which had earned for his country the title of honour: Perfidious Albion.

> H. von Treitschke, 'Europa beim Abschluss des Berliner Vertrags', *Polit. Corr.*, 1879

The English are better traders than manufacturers. The article they produce has no finish, no elegance.

> Max O'Rell [Paul Blouet], *John Bull and His Island*, 1883

London is, indeed, an ignoble mixture of beer and bible, of gin and gospel, of drunkenness and hypocrisy, of unheard-of squalor and unbridled luxury, of misery and prosperity, of poor, abject, shivering, starving creatures, and people insolent with happiness and wealth, whose revenues would appear to us a colossal fortune.

> *ibid.*

Thus we see an Englishman carries everywhere, as the Arab his tent, his English customs, suits, cooking, tea, and habits; his puerilities of detail as well as his favourite hobbies.

> H. France, *John Bull's Army from a French Point of View*, 1887

Ceaseless activity and ruthless competition have for two centuries been the chief characteristics of economic England. ... In England the feeble, the infirm, the timid and the idle are lost.

> E. Boutmy, *Essai d'une psychologie politique du peuple anglais*, 1901

The English belligerent looks on neutral trade as an inconvenience to avoid, a danger to anticipate; to him, commerce is the exception and belligerency the rule.

> *ibid.*

It is because the Englishman is not a gentleman by nature that there is in England a class of gentlemen.

> *ibid.*

It may justly be said that the real English hotel is dear and bad.

Carl Peters, *England and the English*, 1904

English windows open only half-way, either the top half or the bottom half. One may even have the pleasure of opening them a little at the top and a little at the bottom, but not at all in the middle. The sun cannot enter openly, nor the air. The window keeps its selfish and perfidious character. I hate the English windows.

Sarah Bernhardt, *My Double Life*, 1907

It must have been rather a dull society which suffered Beau Brummel for any length of time. It has always been rather an easily amused society, many of them hungry and tired by 8 P.M., preferring physical rather than mental sensations. The two popular stage sensations of the late season, much discussed even by serious men, and patronized by both the smart and the great, were two unclothed women, one interpreting Chopin with her legs, the other representing Buddha with her hips. They were curiously enough both Americans, and I could not help thinking that they must both have died of laughter had they been provided with sleeves to laugh in. To see an English Prime Minister assiduously offering his social patronage to a provider of this quality of entertainment is a feature of English life which leaves the Frenchman, the American, and the German with a bewildering sense that he is either mad or blind.

Price Collier, *England and the English*, 1909

It is generally admitted that in England poverty is looked upon as a crime. This is bound up with class distinction, for every Briton regards himself as king of his little castle, and keeps all others away with warning notices threatening terrible punishment if anyone should dare to enter his domain. Even the squares (rectangular spaces planted with trees) are fenced in and children are only allowed to play there if they live in adjacent houses.

Spiridion Gopčević, *Das Land der unbegrenzten Heuchelei*, 1915

Outside the hotels in London's Strand, and in Covent Garden, at two or three o'clock in the morning, one sees wretches in rags rush to grab the scraps of food which are thrown out. They gnaw the bones clean, as the dogs of Constantinople did in former days. ... It is true that there are workhouses for the poor, where they can get a night's lodging, and where a piece of bread is put in their hand on leaving. But that they have first to earn, by stone-breaking or street-sweeping or rope-making.

ibid.

When in 1066 William the Conqueror with his Normans conquered the Anglo-Saxons at the Battle of Hastings, England fell a prey to those adventurers. The blood-thirsty killed off the natives, the covetous stole their wealth, the lecherous stole their wives and daughters, the soldier helped himself to a house and his commander to a county, and so the robbers became landowners, counts and dukes. That is the origin of the English aristocracy.

ibid.

The British aristocrat of an older generation knew the value of gold, but he also knew the dirt attaching to it. *Non olet* is the slogan of modern mercenary Britain.

W. Franz, *Germanus—Britannien und der Krieg*, 1915 (*see* Coole and Potter, 1941)

England, in these paths, has lowered herself to become a nation of hucksters who have long abandoned the service of God for that of Mammon. Let England's doings be a warning to us Christians.

Pastor J. Rump, 1915 (*see* Coole and Potter, 1941)

The self-controlled English gentleman, who makes un-emotional war out of commercial envy, is more devilish than the Cossack.

O. A. H. Schmitz, 1915 (*ibid.*)

The dreamy habit of mind which comes from solitude in crowds is not fitness for social success in London. England was a social kingdom whose social coinage had no currency elsewhere.

> Henry Adams, *The Education of Henry Adams,*
> 1918 (privately pr. 1907)

Englishwomen, from the educational point of view, could give nothing until they approached forty years old. Then they become very interesting — to the man of fifty.

> *ibid.*

The charm of London which made most impression on Americans was the violence of its contrasts; the extreme badness of the worst, making background for the distinction, refinement or wit of a few, just as the extreme beauty of a few superb women was more effective against the plainness of the crowd. The result was mediaeval and amusing; sometimes coarse to a degree that might have startled a roustabout, and sometimes courteous and considerate to a degree that suggested King Arthur's Round Table.

> *ibid.*

The pirate instinct of the island people interprets economic life very differently. It is a matter of struggle and booty, notably the individual's share of the booty.

> O. Spengler, *Politische Schriften*, 1919 (*see*
> Coole and Potter, 1941)

The British were the first to put under the title, political economy, the theory of *their* plundering world economy. As traders they have been clever enough to know the power of the pen over the people of the most bookish of all civilisations. They persuaded them that the interests of their pirate nation were those of humanity.

> *ibid.*

The electrical economy of Britain is distinguished for its

disintegratedness and backwardness; attempts to nationalise it come up against the opposition of private interests at every step. Not only are the British towns, owing to their historical origins, stupidly planned; all British industry, 'gradually' accumulating, is void of system and plan.

L. Trotsky, *Where is Britain Going?*, 1926.

In England the best people do not earn their own livings. They inherit them. In addition, Englishmen are bred to know their place in society. The best people do not wish to mingle on terms of equality with the lower orders, who must work to support themselves, and the lower orders are acquiescent. Amateurs are known as gentlemen and professionals are known as players, and when, occasionally they do meet in competition, the social demarcation is never forgotten. In the box score the amateur will be Lord Smith, while the professional is just Smith.

Chicago Tribune, 2.i.1928

Mayor William Thompson yesterday received the following cablegram:

'London. Jan. 9. Mayor William Hale Thompson. Greetings. Stated here that an Englishman named Durand in 1810 first developed use of cans for foodstuffs. If so, does not Chicago owe much to that invention? Suggest pleasing gesture if you cable message paying tribute to English inventor, Yorkshire Evening News, 10 Adelphia [*sic!*] Terrace, London, England. (Reply equivalent 1.68 is prepaid.)'

The mayor made public his reply, as follows:

'Answering your cable. I do not know that an Englishman invented tin cans, but I do know that England cornered as usual the tin mines of the world in order to levy tribute out of every person who consumed anything preserved in a tin can.'

Wm. Hale Thompson, *Chicago Tribune*, 8.i.1928

There is something about the attitude of the average English-man towards sex which savours of the most unhappy period in the life of every civilised man. He is an age-long adolescent. . . . The English are sex-starved. They are reluctant to marry, and the chaste bachelor of thirty who so puzzled French observers is not a myth.

> G. J. Renier, *The English: Are they Human?*,
> 1931

There still exists, among the English, a conviction that Scotland Yard is the best detective organisation of the world.

> *ibid.*

Eating and drinking, love-making, and perhaps even the sexual act, clothes, the choice of reading and the organisation of pleasure, the manner of spending a holiday and of killing time in a sea-side boarding-house, conversation, taste, build-ing, and the intercourse between human beings and animals, are regulated by ritual. Throughout the day, the Englishman performs acts and pronounces words, not because they have a significance in themselves, but because they happen to be the acts and words which, for one reason or another, it is deemed right to perform and to pronounce.

> *ibid.*

It seems to me that the main contact of the bulk of the English nation with sport consists in looking on and betting.

> *ibid.*

A man from the Continent gives himself an air of importance by talking: an Englishman by holding his tongue.

> Karel Čapek, *Letters from England*, 1932

The horrible thing in East London is not what can be seen and smelt, but its unbounded and unredeemable extent. Elsewhere poverty and ugliness exist merely as a rubbish-heap between two houses, like an unsavoury nook, a cess-pool or unclean offal; but here there are miles and miles of grimy houses, hopeless streets, Jewish shops, a superfluity of children, gin palaces and Christian shelters.

ibid.

At Exeter I was beset by an English Sunday coupled with rain. An Exeter Sunday is so thorough and holy that the very churches are closed, and as regards creature comforts, the way-farer who despises cold potatoes must go to bed with an empty stomach; I do not know what particular joy this causes to the Exeter God.

ibid.

Lovers carry on their love-making in the parks heavily, morosely and without a word. Drinkers drink in bars, each by himself.

ibid.

The English retailer is concerned with maintaining his dignity rather than with selling his goods.

C. Hansen, *The English Smile*, 1935

The hideous, lying body of action that is England's industrial cities, England's empire.

Waldo Frank, *The Bridegroom Cometh*, 1938

Well, to be perfectly frank about it, the disadvantages of English life (which I accepted with such jovial tolerance when I was reading about them in New York) are beginning to hit a little closer home. It is so damp! I wear a light coat indoors and a heavy one outside, and yet it still seems to me that I can almost feel the mould forming on my face and hands. We are much invited out and we take our meals everywhere—in other hostels, in restaurants and in private houses. I was well warned about English food, so it did not surprise me, but I do wonder, sometimes, how they ever manage to prise it up long enough to get a plate under it.

M. Halsey, *With Malice toward Some*, 1938

London stores are not imposing. Most of their window displays look like jungles and even the pared-down ones lack intuition and rightness. And their idea of a well-turned out woman is something resembling a Biblical character in a charade.

ibid.

The English hotels we have stayed in so far always seemed to me expressly planned to discourage people from remaining away from home overnight. The red plush. The black walnut. The framed engravings of lovers' quarrels. The Pampas grass. The fireplace blocked up with nasty little brutes of gas heaters. Whenever we checked out of a hotel this summer, it was with the moral certainty that the manager immediately retired to his office for a few minutes of private rejoicing. 'There', he would say, looking out of his window after us, 'that'll teach 'em to go gadding about!'

ibid.

In middle-class England a woman is offered a drink with the same degree of frequency with which she is offered deadly nightshade, and at English dinners, when it gets on for ten o'clock and you are numb with cold and half hysterical from hearing about English weather, the gentlemen all have whisky-and-soda and the ladies, God bless them, have tea! A woman who wants hard liquor at an English dinner has to ask for it, and then her host (nice and warm himself, of course, in woollen clothes, long sleeves and the radiation from a quantity of port) glances questioningly at her husband, as who should say, 'She's a little minx, but I don't believe a tiny bit would hurt her.' It is a discouraging state of affairs, for (quite aside from the cold storage dining) probably no class of people in the world could do more handily with a little of the stimulation and release of alcohol than well-bred Englishwomen. However, a visiting American does better to refrain from proselytising, to do her drinking in large batches (if possible) on the maid's day out, and on other occasions to remain silent and stoically let the pleurisy fall where it may.

ibid.

English life is seven-eighths below the surface, like an iceberg, and living in England for a year constitutes merely an introduction to an introduction to an introduction to it.

ibid.

The compelling tradition of social decency is so great that all you need to do to make an Englishman a gentleman again is to ship him back west of the Suez Canal. Really the white man is quite charming when he has got rid of his 'burden'.

Lin Yutang, *Between Tears and Laughter*, 1945

When I visited England in 1935 British girls had less freedom than most of their continental sisters. The average English girl went through the school her parents could afford, and picked out. There she studied the limited number of subjects considered 'best' for her. That included everything that makes for a good housekeeper, and very little more. Generally, jobs were practically closed to girls. The working girl was frowned upon, and her pay and professional standing were below those of her male colleagues.

The ultimate, respectable aim for every English girl was to become a faithful and obedient servant to a suitable husband, so that the latter could live happily ever after. Her one important function, besides bearing children, was pouring the tea for hubby and guests.

Fred Hechinger, *Washington Post*, 11.viii.1946

The upper-class Englishman is so retiring that he seems hardly to be in the room with you at all.

Emily Hahn, *Meet the British*, 1953

The nation is hypnotized by flickering flames. Some people use marihuana, some opium, some alcohol, but the British are pyromaniacs. 'There's something about an open fire,' they say. And so there is. Look at cats and dogs, if you don't believe me, comatose in their addiction, staring into the flames. You can grow quite goofy, sitting at a fire.

ibid.

No land is so beautiful, no people live so comfortably, none can so overwhelm one so completely with interest and hospitality, but the main purpose is never forgotten. The subtlety and skill of English propaganda methods are just becoming apparent to us cruder Americans.

Porter Sargent, *Between Two Wars: The Failure of Education, 1920–40,* 1945

On a fine day the climate of England is like looking up a chimney; on a foul day, like looking down one.

Anon.

Politics

L'Angleterre, ah! la perfide Angleterre.
Bossuet, 1652

Will you allow these revelling goddams, gross swillers of ale, lackeys and hen-stealers, to share in the heritage of France?
Invective sur l'erreur pusillanime et lâcheté des gens d'armes de France, 16th cent.

It is believed in England that the English bow-men could, in a few years, conquer the whole of Africa.
De Puebla to King Ferdinand, 5.x.1507

The kingdom on the other hand is no less sufficient for its own defence than feeble for offensive operations, with the exception of plundering at sea (of which the French are always in dread from the English) and disembarking and burning a few villages.
G. Micheli, Report to Venetian Senate, 1557

. . . rabid hatred of the English for the Spaniards and (as a natural consequence) for all other foreigners.
ibid.

The enterprise of expelling the Queen of England and mastering the realms presents no great difficulty, for it has little money, few fighting men and not a single fortress; while it is torn by strife between Catholics and heretics. The difficulty

169

consists in the antagonism between the humours; for the English cannot endure the rule of foreigners.

Nicholas Ormanetto, bishop of Padua, 18.ix.1572

I am, however, truly of opinion, that the king and queen of England are better off at St Germain than in their perfidious kingdom.

Mme de Sévigné, letter to Mme de Grignan, 1689

Haughty republicans, vain tyrants of Neptune,
Warding off storms and braving misfortunes,
You merely follow a blind courage,
And crime you add to infamous outrage.
And so all honour, freedom and equity,
Are silenced today by your violence and iniquity.

Lefebvre de Beauvray, *Adresse à la Nation
anglaise*, 1757

I would rather be in dependence on Great Britain, properly limited, than on any nation on earth, or than on no nation. But I am one of those, too, who, rather than submit to the rights of legislating for us, assumed by the British Parliament, and which late experience has shown they will so cruelly exercise, would lend my hand to sink the whole island in the ocean.

Thomas Jefferson to John Randolph, August,
1775

If ever a nation was mad and foolish, blind to its own interests, and bent on its own destruction, it is Britain. There are such things as national sins, and though the punishment of individuals may be reserved to another world, national punishment can only be inflicted in this world. Britain, as a nation, is in my inmost belief, the greatest and most ungrateful offender against God on the face of the whole earth. Blessed with all the commerce she could wish for, and furnished by the vast extent of the dominion with the means of civilising both the eastern and western world, she has made no use of both, than proudly to idolize her own 'thunder' and rip up the bowels of whole countries, for what she could get. Like Alexander, she has made war for sport, and inflicted misery for prodigality's sake. The blood of India is not yet repaid nor the wretchedness of Africa yet requited. Of late, she has enlarged her list of national cruelties, by the butcherly destruction of the Caribbs of St Vincent's and in returning an answer by the sword, to the meek prayers for 'peace, liberty and safety'.

Thomas Paine, letter to Lord Howe in *Common Sense*, 13.i.1777 (*see The American Crisis*, 1792)

Her idea of national honour seems to consist in national insult; and that to be a great people, is to be neither a Christian, a philosopher, nor a gentleman, but to threaten with the rudeness of a bear, and to devour with the ferocity of a lion.

T. Paine,[1] *A letter to the people of England* (*Common Sense*, 21.xi.1778, *ibid.*)

The arm of Britain has been spoken of as the arm of the Almighty, and she has lived of late, as if she thought the whole world created for her diversion. Her politics, instead of civilising, have tended to brutalise mankind, and under the title of DEFENDER OF THE FAITH she has made war like an Indian against the religion of humanity.

ibid.

They are like sick men, who have had a violent fever and do not realise their condition until the attack is past.

Frederick the Great, August, 1784

A nation, whose thirst for domination and wealth has produced, to the ruin of all parts of the globe, systems of oppression and crimes which would have revolted the Romans, those past masters of brigandage; a nation which hunts liberty as a rival.

Mirabeau, *Aux Bataves . . .*, 1788

---

[1] Paine, although an Englishman, gives a classic statement of the American viewpoint.

British speculators, dealers in treason and slaves, bankers in crimes and counter-revolutionaries, we detest tyranny, because we abhor you. The hatred of Rome for Carthage thrives again in French souls, just as Punic faith lives again in English hearts.

> Bertrand Barère, *Rapport fait à la Convention Nationale . . . sur les crimes d'Angleterre*, 1794

There exists among the nations, among all societies of men, a kind of natural law, known as the law of human rights, but it is unknown to the natives policed by Great Britain; she is a tribe foreign to Europe, foreign to humanity; she must be obliterated.

> *ibid.*

Its favourite plan is to corrupt the human species, or to kill off one part so as to enslave the other.

> *ibid.*

It is no wonder that Great Britain is worse governed than if it were under the rule of a German prince bishop. English politics lack all system, and are so completely devoid of all plan and purpose, that one is tempted to believe that in England all depends on the whims and passions of the ruling minister, who just consults his own opinions, and carries them out by sacrificing the blood and wealth of his country.

> A. Riem, *Reise durch England*, 1798–9

It is certainly not the fault of the British government that manufacturing and trade did not completely die out at a time when the utmost was being done to improve them. With a folly unequalled in the history of any nation, the British government favoured increase of trade and yet crushed it with unheard-of taxation.

> *ibid.*

The Englishman nurses petty prejudices against his fellow-citizens in Wales; he despises the Scotsman; he hates and persecutes the Irish. In the East and West Indies he watches with indifference the annihilation of millions; and the most shameful extortions move him but little, or he would punish the villainous nabobs.

ibid.

No country has had so many revolutions as England. They were never fortunate enough to possess the firmness of character and courage necessary to repel the attacks of their enemies. After being subdued by the Romans, they soon succumbed to the domination of the Normans, Saxons, etc. Then they changed the succession, created parties, like those of York and Lancaster, bowed down to the usurper Henry V, banished the Stuarts; then they submitted to Charles II, and banished James II; took the sinister William of Orange for a king; subjected themselves to the house of Hannover, and were even prepared to put the Stuarts again on the throne, if the battle of Cullodon had had a different outcome, and are at present content that the house of Hannover has turned their government into a despotic one. They imagined they had a free constitution, but their Henrys, Edwards, Cromwells, Charles, Williams and Georges convinced them otherwise, by turning their constitution into a rudder of despotism and deluding the people into believing they were tyrannising themselves.

ibid.

Here one finds in the unbridled dishonesty of the ministers, in the enormous orgies of the landed gentry, in the large-scale bribery of governments, in the extremes of covetousness, in the unbelievable tyranny of the government and the priesthood; in the murderous sacrifice of countless thousands to selfishness and intolerance; in the ever-ready breaking of treaties and alliances; in the utterly senseless frittering of public monies; in the crippling taxation of the poor; in their most inhuman treatment of the unfortunates in public institutions; in the barbaric ignorance in the universities and other places of education; in the highly ridiculous displays of wealth and arrogance; in the most revolting eccentricities, in short, in everything which would be a stigma in other countries, one finds—no shame at all.

ibid.

All the efforts of England to appear a great nation were based on such foolish principles that they have contributed to its downfall. North and Pitt turned the might of Britain into a meteor, which gleams and then fades. And even this power was only partly derived, and acquired by purchase.

ibid.

The English government is an arrant egoist, a cosmopolitan pirate, a hostile trader, whose country is anywhere where crimes and gold are to be found. Wherever you find commercial invasion, usurpation of colonies, barbarous behaviour, civil war, continental war, and political or religious assassinations, it will be by the perfidious hand of the English government.

Bertrand Barère, *La Liberté des Mers*, 1798

The English government behaves as a conqueror, plies the seas as a pirate, colonises like a despot, deals as a merchant, administers as a tyrant, and negotiates like a master.

ibid.

Aux armes, citoyens, que le perfide anglais
Bientôt, bientôt n'ait qu'à choisir sa ruine ou la Paix.

Refrain of new words to the tune of
La Marseillaise, n.d.

Hypocritical enemies of the peace of Europe, constant fomenters of war. Europe never believes you when you talk of peace.

[Bertrand Barère], *Lettre Ouverte d'un Citoyen*
Français en réponse à Lord Grenville, 1800

If Europe has to maintain her military attitude, under the influence of the English government, she can only expect to be dominated by the tyranny of force, naval brigandage, the ferocity of northern barbarians, the insatiable greed of commercial gain, universal venality, Machiavellism of governments, political corruption, spread of Punic faith, and legislation at once oppressive, fiscal, obscure and inquisitorial, reviving a military feudalism: that is the kind of security offered to Europe by continuous war waged by the English government.

ibid.

Britain with her merchant fleet
Her tentacles extends,
And all the realm of Amphitrite
She claims for her own ends.

F. von Schiller, 1801

Tremble, odious England, your cup is full. Tremble! fear the blows which indignant France will aim at you: they will be as terrible as thunder. Cries for vengeance are making themselves heard. Distraught mothers demand from you their children, dead victims of your ambition. Warriors mutilated for you, yet which you had not the loyalty to include in your treaties of exchange, call for eternal justice against your perfidy. Their prayers shall be answered: you will fall, and the avenged world will hasten to applaud your downfall.

J. Diacon, *Guerre à l'Angleterre,* 1802

And so England, by her insolent egoism, her turbulent policy, tyrannical diplomacy, limitless ambition and horrible perfidy, alienated herself from European affairs and was driven from the Continent. By perpetual violation of the rights of man and treaties, she has become an object of odium to the Continental powers.

Observations sur le manifeste du roi d'Angleterre,
1803

What! Shall of Albion the infernal puissance
In fearful frenzy lord it over France,
The better to bend Europe to her will?
And shall she dominate o'er ocean wave,
And under homicidal laws enslave
　　　　Neptune still?

No, no! Whatever scourge the war shall bring,
And England's dread array before us fling,
Yet never shall her leopards cause us fear;
Her party spirit, gross licentiousness,
Her hatred, crimes, unworthy vengefulness
      Bring her end near.

These haughty vandals, illfam'd island race,
Transgressing bounds of virtue and of grace,
Despiting honour, claim the name of great;
But they, so proud of their philosophy,
And scorning precepts of philanthropy,
      Are pirate state.

So often have we seen their roving fleet,
Thronging with arrogance the mighty deep,
Spreading terror, beguiling men with words.
'The ocean', they say, 'is *our* heritage,
The *English* shall it rule from age to age,
      They are its lords.'

(There are 21 other stanzas in this vein.)
Ode aux Français, par P.C., Citoyen de Millau,
1804

Your fall will come about by no fault but your own, if you do not mend your ways. Vulgar contempt for what is noblest, the rating of everything in terms of gold, the estimation of nations according to their wealth, the suppression of the poor and the arrogance of your nabobs—all this will sound your death knell. A people which despises everything beautiful and great if it happens to be of foreign origin, which despite all education can only see paradise in Old England and barbarity everywhere else, in short, a people that can no longer invent or produce anything original, but in mean and miserly fashion piles up for show what more illustrious ancestors invented and created—if such a stubborn and sclerotic people does not become slavish and commonplace, then the portents of history lie. . . .

England will not be destroyed by war, but, like other

nations, by its own crimes and wickedness. Arrogant insulars, when there is no longer a nabob to tax or a land to plunder, when you have more venal merchants than buyers, when there is no longer a free voice to sound for the old constitution and wretched slaves bleat their 'Britannia rules the waves' out of hoarse throats—then, thrown back on your own resources, your shame and your self-made misery—you will know yourselves exasperated but be too weak to rise again for the sake of past glory. Then the world will see the final fall of Britain.

M. Arndt, 'Engländer', *Geist der Zeit*, 1805

The British government presents the singular phenomenon of a nation, the individuals of which are as faithful to their private engagements and duties, as honorable, as worthy, as those of any nation on earth, and whose government is yet the most unprincipled at this day known.

Thomas Jefferson, 1810

I consider the government of England as totally without morality, insolent beyond bearing, inflated with vanity and ambition, aiming at the exclusive domination of the sea, lost in corruption, of deep-rooted hatred towards us, hostile to Liberty wherever it endeavours to show its head, and the eternal disturber of the peace of the world.

Thomas Jefferson to Thomas Leiper, June 1815

In England, everything revolves round the upper classes. Everything is done by and for them. . . . It is members of the English aristocratic families who make all the laws, because all the most important institutions have been founded by them. They hold most of the important posts. No one complains of the way in which the law is administered, because it only exists to keep the rabble in order.

Napoleon, 9.ii.1821 (*see Napoleon at St Helena: Memoirs of General Bertrand*, ed. Fleuriot, transl. F. Hume, 1953)

One of these days John Bull will turn against the English ruling classes and he will hang the lot. I shall not be there to see it, but you will. You will have an even more terrible revolution than ours.

> Napoleon, 13.iv.1821, conversation with
> Dr Arnott (*ibid.*)

The Emperor stated that he died murdered by the English Ruling Class and its hired assassins.

> Napoleon, 22.iv.1821, conversation with
> Grand Marshal (*ibid.*)

Napoleon remarked that England was badly governed. Given her commercial resources, had he been governing England the people would not have a farthing of tax to pay, whereas actually taxation was breaking them. They were the most miserable of people.

> Napoleon, 23.iv.1821, conversation with
> doctors (*ibid.*)

But though we cannot with justice cast any imputation on England for the change which she made in the choice of her allies (if she erred in that, she committed political errors, for which she would have to atone)—the non-performance of engagements for which she had made herself responsible certainly exposes her to merited censure. In the three great continental wars in which England took part, the Spanish, the Austrian war of succession, and the seven years' war, she concluded every time a peace for herself, or only in connection with Holland, and deserted her principal confederates. This conduct did not originate in any refined policy, systematically taken up, nor in a dereliction of public faith and confidence, but in the change of political principles, which, according to the general spirit of the British constitution, is almost inseparably connected with a change of ministry. . . . Hence arises, what is certainly a most pernicious consequence in respect to foreign powers, that the British government cannot guarantee with the same assurance as others, the performance of its obligation.

> A. H. L. Heeren, *The rise and growth of the*
> *continental interests of Great Britain*, 1821
> (transl. 1836)

While the Germans are tormenting themselves with philosophical problems, the English, with their great practical understanding, laugh at us and win the world.

> J. W. von Goethe, September 1829 (*see*
> J. P. Eckermann, *Gespräche mit Goethe* . . .)
> *1823–32*, 1836–8

I do not think of egoistical England as a fat, prosperous beer paunch, as shown in caricatures, but as described by a satirist, as a tall, thin, bony old bachelor, who is sewing a missing button on his trousers with linen thread, at the end of which hangs, as a ball of thread, the world—and he calmly cuts off the thread he doesn't want, and just lets the world fall into the abyss.

> H. Heine, *Französische Zustände*, 1832

Do not be surprised at this aversion, still strong in the English, for everything approaching generalisation, synthesis, and one might say spiritualism, and do not be surprised at the egoism of which we complain; these are the logical consequences of a life founded on Protestantism in morals, and on a principle of liberty alone, not harmonised by equality and social union. From Protestantism comes a habit of bare and paltry analysis; from an edifice based on liberty alone springs naturally individualism, and from the utmost development of analysis and individualism spring materialism and egoism. The English are now at this point; however, they are approaching, slowly as usual, but fatally and inevitably, a revolution which will be tremendous, like all revolutions of equality, which are social and not political.

> G. Mazzini to G. E. Benza, 7.iii.1839, *Letters*
> (transl. A. de Rosen Jervis, 1930)

But we would not like to send you [Guizot] back to London as ambassador; that needs someone with a hawk's eye, who can spy out the tricks of Perfidious Albion in good time, or a rough, uneducated fellow, who will have no intellectual sympathy with the government of Great Britain, cannot make polite speeches in English, but will answer bluntly in French when they fob him off with equivocal statements.

H. Heine, *Lutezia*, 1840

All our wars came to us from England. Never would she listen to any proposal for peace. Did she then believe that the Emperor Napoleon wished her ruin? Such a thought was never harboured in his mind.

Prince L.-N. Bonaparte, *On the opinions and Policy of Napoleon*, 1840

One can estimate, throughout this history, the evil done to us by England's financial system, allied to its politics, and becoming its most formidable weapon. We have seen how, throughout the duration of the revolution and the Empire, this power, strong in resources for making money out of everything in the world, constantly offering funds to the European sovereigns for arms against France, inciting them to war while signing peace treaties, making them fight one after another until finally mustering them all together, assisted by the elements, by the very faults of her adversary, and finally by the supreme, perfidious weapon of treason, at last succeeded in overcoming her enemy. Was not this colossal overthrow a bad thing for humanity? To lower all the flags of Europe before the Cossacks—was that an act worthy of a free people? God has already replied to this question with distant thunder of revolutions which threaten the English ruling classes.

L. P. E. Bignon, *Histoire de France*, XIV, 1850

A thousand examples prove that England has converted every treaty to her own profit, whether by the skilful interpretation of her diplomatists, or the rapid intervention of her admirals.

A. A. de Ledru-Rollin, *De la Décadence de l'Angleterre*, 1850

As to the right of neutrals, why, the ocean bears testimony, on all its coasts, to the brigandage of England; ports burned, vessels captured, flags insulted, cargoes pillaged or sequestered,

crews surprised and stowed down below, when not massacred
—such, in all times, has been her exploits.

ibid.

People, living near together like the English, and inhabiting
the same country, know as little of each other as if the sea
rolled between them. . . . If such a state of ignorance exists
among the population of a country like England, as to the
character, conditions, feelings, and wants of its several orders,
we may cease to wonder that so little was formerly known of
the colonies, by those whose interest and duty it was to inform
themselves.

Rule and Mis-rule of the English in America, by
the author of 'Sam Slick the Clockmaker', 1851

It is a crazy doctrine, widely preached in England, that
discipline, law, order, responsibility, all the real guarantees
that wisdom and time have created, should be sacrificed for
imaginary control of an imaginary thing—public opinion.

Lothar Bucher, *Der Parlamentarismus wie er ist*,
1855

By your declaring yourselves hostile to any national movement, . . . by your renouncing every moral aim, every noble
aspiration, for a paltry programme of expediency and *status
quo*, you have deprived yourselves of the sympathies of all the
good and brave throughout Europe.

G. Mazzini, *Two letters to the People of England
on the War*, 1855 (transl. A. de Rosen Jervis)

The same insular limitation pinches his foreign politics. He
sticks to his traditions and usages, and so help him God! he
will force his island by-laws down the throat of great
countries, like India, China, Canada, Australia, and not only
so, but impose Wapping on the Congress of Vienna, and
trample down all nationalities with his taxed boots. Lord
Chatham goes for liberty, and no taxation without representation—for that is British law; but not a hobnail shall they dare
make in America, but buy their nails in England—for that also

is British law; and the fact that British commerce was to be re-created by the independence of America, took them all by surprise.

R. W. Emerson, *English Traits*, 1856

The foreign policy of England, though ambitious and lavish of money, has not often been generous or just. It has a principal regard to the interest of trade, checked, however, by the aristocratic bias of the ambassador, which usually puts him in sympathy with the continental courts. It sanctioned the partition of Poland, it betrayed Genoa, Sicily, Parga, Greece, Turkey, Rome and Hungary.

ibid.

England calmly pocketed every shame it could wrest from its neighbours. Ah well, all firebrands turn at last to ashes.

F. Grillparzer, *Sprüche und Epigramme*, 1856

The English proletariat is getting more and more bourgeois, so that this most bourgeois of all nations is seemingly aiming at a bourgeois aristocracy and a bourgeois proletariat, as well as a bourgeoisie. This is not entirely unjustifiable for a nation which seeks to exploit the whole world.

F. Engels to Marx, Oct. 1858

The Fourth of July each year, the anniversary of the Declaration of Independence, was observed with military honours in every city, town and village up to the time that the late civil war began. On that day the Revolutionary ardour of the people, maintained lukewarmly during the year by the pictures of battles with the British and by the portraits of Washington which adorn every house, was allowed full and ample vent. The militia were paraded; the survivors of 1776 and 1812 were feasted and escorted in processions; fireworks were displayed, cannon fired, and bells rung; and from one end of the land to the other there was a general jubilation. At every gathering public speakers, more or less eloquent, bearded the British lion in his den, dragged him from his lair, trotted him up and down before the people, exposed his weaknesses as compared with the increasing might of the American eagle, and only refrained from turning the poor animal inside out, and tearing him to pieces, oratorically, upon condition that he would behave himself better in future. This exhibition was often laughable; but it had its uses, and it has its moral. Before the rebellion of 1861, the Americans had begun to see its comical side. They are too good-natured and too conscious of their own strength to bear malice, and their sense of humour is so keen that they laugh at themselves as readily as at other people. Since the British lion offered no resistance, and made no reply to the taunts and invectives of the oratorical Womb-wells and Van Amburghs, it became rather a bore to see him so hauled about and roughly treated. Consequently the popular liking for this feature of the celebration visibly diminished, and the old style of the Fourth-of-July speakers found themselves chaffed, guyed, burlesqued, and caricatured by their own countrymen. During the Civil War, the lion of England disappeared from the Fourth-of-July exhibition almost entirely. . . . When the Union is firmly re-established the old custom will be revived, however; the national menagerie, composed of the British lion and the American eagle, will be again exhibited, and the performance will proceed as usual, until it shall again be mollified and abbreviated by more important events.

[Stephen Fiske], *English Photographs,*
By an American, 1869

However highly one may think of British liberty, England today is undoubtedly a reactionary force in the society of nations. Her position in the world is an obvious anachronism. It was created in those good old days, when world wars were still decided by naval battles and mercenaries, and it was thought politic in the dominating countries to seize by force strategically situated naval bases, without any regard to natural or historical rights. In an era of national states and great armies, this kind of cosmopolitan trading nation can no longer continue to assert itself; the time will and must come when Gibraltar will belong to the Spaniards, Malta to the

Italians, Heligoland to the Germans, and the Mediterranean to the Mediterranean peoples.

> H. von Treitschke, *Die Türkei und die Grossmächte,*
> 1876

England is today the shameless protagonist of barbarism in international law. It is her fault that naval warfare still retains the character of privileged piracy, to the disgrace of all mankind. At the Brussels Conferences her opposition frustrated the attempt of Germany and Russia to set some limits to the depredations of land warfare.

> *ibid.*

Our faithful ally continues with its perfidious and tortuous policy, . . . trying by all means to absorb the commerce of that part of the world [Africa]. This our faithful ally is insatiable, and when it treats of gold and profit, it values its friends no more than its enemies.

> A. Fernandez de los Rios, *Mi Mision en Portugal,*
> 1877 (citing *Diario Progresista,* 28.x.1876)

The complications of the Irish land problem . . . are so great that the easy way to solve it would be to give the Irish Home Rule and let them solve it themselves. But John Bull is too stupid to understand this.

> Karl Marx to Jenny Longuet, April 1881

Magnanimity, in politics especially, is a virtue of which John Bull claims the sole monopoly.

> Max O'Rell [Paul Blouet], *John Bull and His*
> *Island,* 1883

It is the English, with their absurd policies, who are ruining trade on all these coasts. They insist on altering everything, and have ended by doing worse than the Egyptians and Turks whom they have ruined. Their Gordon is an idiot, their Wolseley an ass, and all their undertakings just a mad succession of acts of folly and plunder.

> A. Rimbaud, letter from Aden, Dec. 1884

Victory! With them it is always victory—victory all along the line.

I was surprised, in perusing their school histories, to learn that they had always beaten us soundly in every encounter; that they alone had undertaken, conducted, and ended the Crimean War, while we merely looked on. You would simply astound the rising generation of Cockneys if you informed them that to the Germans belongs the so much vaunted glory of Waterloo.

> Hector France, *John Bull's Army from a French
> Point of View*, 1887

These people have neither the will nor the power to fire a gun. Their game is completely Machiavellian, and whoever gets involved with them will soon repent it.

> Metternich, 6.ii.1836, recorded in *Souvenirs du
> baron de Barante . . . 1782–1866*, 1890–1901

She likes to censure and even insult the strong, to justify and encourage the weak; but it seems that she does not care to go further than assume virtuous airs and discuss honourable theories. Should her protégés need her help she offers her moral support.

> A. de Tocqueville, *Souvenirs*, 1893

England as a world power has been actuated solely by her own interests, and has pursued them with the ruthlessness of the most blatant egoism. The friendship and devotion which even a nation could find in a neighbour by unselfish help have always been despised by the English; in their politics they have always managed their affairs strictly through their pockets, and the advances they have occasionally made in special circumstances have always been motivated by and based on *do ut*. We Germans have least reason to be grateful to the English, rather have we the most serious and weighty reasons to look on them as incorrigible Danai, as soon as they begin paying any attention to us.

> *Our English Friends. Eine deutsche Antwort auf
> englische Unverschämtheiten*, 1895

History teaches us that no reliance can be placed upon England, and the present general political situation must convince the most *bona fide* Anglophile that England is now less than ever capable of alliance with us. The essence of English policy has always been to be good friends only with those who can be of use to her.

ibid.

Chamberlain always seems to me like the giant in an English picture-book that I once had, who withdrew into a cave, hung up his boots outside, went in and said (as far as I can remember), 'The man who wants these boots to steal—must first to my strength appeal.' Englishmen do not drink as much as they used, and their politics have likewise deteriorated.

Bismarck to *Neue Freie Presse* correspondent,
August 1897

Sorry am I to regard the English nation, in its political and official actions towards my own people, and in the conduct of many of its representatives in South Africa, as our ancient, inveterate enemy, arrogant, covetous, unscrupulous, aye, shameless and insolent, in practices of iniquity to our hurt and damage. We have done no wrong to that old enemy, but here he is again. Because it turns out, of late years, that this country north of the Vaal, which has been ours for half a century, includes rich gold-fields, he will not allow our Republic to stand any longer.

C. N. J. Du Plessis, *The Transvaal Boer speaking for himself* (tr. R. Acton), 1899

England is the international world power which threatens all independence, all nationality, a new Rome, which destroys, crushes, strangles nationality and individuality.

Die Hilfe, March 1900

They have never treated a conquered people as their equals, nor understood how to conciliate them. Their method has always been to oppress them, exploit them, crush or destroy them.

E. Boutmy, *Essai d'une Psychologie politique du Peuple Anglais*, 1901

The law in England is largely a matter of opinion of more or less ancient date.

ibid.

Loyalty, veracity, humanity, and generosity towards the weak they believe to be 'truth on this side of the Channel, error on the other'.

ibid.

England always remains true to herself: she makes assertions, and so soon as she is given the opportunity of convincing herself of their inaccuracy, resorts to cowardly and insipid evasions, but at the same time repeats her assertions, until she herself, and sometimes the world with her, begins to believe in their truth.

P. Kruger, *Memoirs* (tr. A. T. de Mattos), 1902

As soon as it suited her convenience, perfidious Albion broke her peaceful promise, as she always has done and as she will always continue to whenever it serves her purpose.

ibid.

How typically English was this conduct on the part of a high-placed British official. It is characteristic of the entire English policy in South Africa. Lies, treachery, intrigues and secret instigations against the Government of the Republic: these have always been the distinguishing marks of English politics, which found their final goal in this present cruel war.

ibid.

A distorted view of English history, in which Great Britain figures as the apex of human development towering high above all other nations, stamps on the minds of the young that insular arrogance which forms the nation's worst characteristic.

C. Peters, *England and the English*, 1904

England is almost entirely to blame for the evils which have made Spain one of the most wretched countries on earth. If it were not for the English pirates . . . and certain events in which Great Britain, intent on her own commercial advantages, has always played so large a part, Spain today would be a rich and powerful nation.

J. Just Lloret, *Inglaterra Arbitra de España!*,
1906

We have more to fear from British diplomats than British dreadnoughts.

Senator Hitchcock, 1912

The genuineness of the courtesy, the real kindness and the hospitality of the English are beyond praise and without limit. In this they show a strange contradiction to their dickering habits in trade and their 'unctuous rectitude' in stealing continents. I know a place in the world now where they are steadily moving their boundary line into other people's territory. I guess they really believe that the earth belongs to them.

Ambassador W. Page to Herbert S. Houston,
1913

HYMN OF HATE

French and Russian they matter not,
A blow for a blow and a shot for a shot;
We love them not, we hate them not,
We hold the Weichsel and Vosges-gate,
We have but one and only hate,
We love as one, we hate as one,
We have one foe and one alone.

He is known to you all, he is known to you all,
He crouches behind the dark grey flood,
Full of envy, of rage, of craft, of gall,
Cut off by waves that are thicker than blood.
Come, let us stand at the Judgment place,
An oath to swear to, face to face,
An oath of bronze no wind can shake,
An oath for our sons and their sons to take.

Come, hear the word, repeat the word,
Throughout the Fatherland make it heard.
We will never forgo our hate,
We have all but a single hate,
We love as one, we hate as one,
We have one foe, and one alone—
    ENGLAND!

In the Captain's mess, in the banquet-hall,
Sat feasting the officers one and all,
Like a sabre-blow, like the swing of a sail,
One seized his glass held high to hail;
Sharp-snapped like the stroke of a rudder's play,
Spoke three words only: 'To the Day!'
Whose glass this fate?
They had all but a single hate.
Who was thus known?
They had one foe and one alone—
    ENGLAND!

Take you the folk of the earth in pay,
With bars of gold your ramparts lay,
Bedeck the ocean with bow on bow,
Ye reckon well, but not well enough now.
French and Russian they matter not,
A blow for a blow, a shot for a shot,
We fight the battle with bronze and steel.
And the time that is coming, peace will seal.

You will hate with a lasting hate,
We will never forgo our hate,
Hate by water and hate by land,
Hate of the head and hate of the hand,
Hate of the hammer and hate of the crown,
Hate of seventy millions, choking down,
We love as one, we hate as one,
We have one foe and one alone—
    ENGLAND!
        Ernst Lissauer, 1914 (*see* Coole and Potter, 1941)

England's commercial enmity has now . . . unleashed the greatest war the world has ever seen. As the English could not do anything to equal us in scientific thought, assiduous commerce, in discipline, the source of our organisation, as we have surpassed them in the iron and steel industry, the chemical industry and so many others, they have kindled this war against us.

Alois Riehl, lecture, Oct. 1914 (ibid.)

Think on this as long as you live, and pass it on to the coming generation: that they should devote all their energies and their last pfennig to building up the German fleet and every other means to attain one end and one end only:

DOWN WITH ENGLAND!

Admiral zu der Valois, Nieder mit England, 1915

Fundamentally, Britain is responsible for this war. She was jealous. British businessmen wanted it—it is a British business war. . . . We feel no enmity towards France or Russia, and we think highly of the French. But Britain! We hate Britain!

Hindenburg, interview with Senator Beveridge,
1915

England is a moloch that will devour anything, a vampire that will suck tribute from all the veins of the earth, a monster snake, encircling the whole equator. . . . To tear the cruel world sceptre out of England's hands is the great task for the people of the earth. It is world judgment which must be fulfilled by world history.

Pastor Tolzien, Vaterländische Kriegsvorträge, 1915
(see Coole and Potter, 1941)

And how badly commercial and political England is now abusing the truth. The lie, impudent, shameless and cynical, more so than ever, has become a recognised weapon of attack, handled with virtuosity.

W. Franz, Britannien und der Krieg, 1915 (ibid.)

Although the British sailor has retained the cunning and unscrupulousness of the pirate, lying in wait for neutral cargo vessels, laying mines in the waters of neighbour countries not participating in the war, and committing acts of violence of the most diverse kinds, he lacks the pirate's determination and daring in attack.

ibid.

The English of those days were not supermen. In the age of discovery they discovered nothing, in the age of invention they invented nothing. But they did know how to plough with other peoples' oxen, and what distinguished them from all the other European nations, was the energy engendered by their greed.

Count Ernst zu Reventlow, *Der Vampir des Festlandes*, 1915

Through the whole of English history, and up to the present day, one can see the repeated use of three methods: the first is the destruction of the means by which the nation to be plundered protects its property on the seas and overseas, i.e. the destruction of its fleet, harbours, docks, etc.; the second is the seizure or destruction of its trading vessels. When these aims have been more or less realised, the robber seizes its overseas possessions.

ibid.

Now we know that the English gentleman is a myth, and that what we took to be inner nobility and genuine culture is really a calculated pose, deliberately adopted for reasons of expedience. Our own bitter experience has thus opened our eyes to the lessons of English history, which shows perfidious Albion to be pursuing the most ruthless policy of self-interest, dictated by the most unscrupulous greed for power and gain that the world has ever known. The method of sheer iron logic, by which the English people bring their search for power and gain to a successful conclusion, would wring from us icy admiration, if their persistent efforts to hide a selfish rapacity under a cloak of morality and idealism did not arouse our disgust at this masterly hypocrisy, which has earned for England the name of 'Perfidious Albion'.

Alfred Geiser, *Das perfide Albion*, 1915

Great Britain is not to be blamed for making the best terms she can in her diplomatic bargaining. We should admire the ability with which she has overreached us. Let us not waste strength in resenting it, but betake ourselves to learning how she does it. . . . While in statesmanship we have little to learn from Great Britain—not so much perhaps as she has to learn from us—in diplomacy we cannot do better than to go to school to her. We should be thankful that we have not suffered more from our inferiority to her than we have.

> J. Bigelow, *Breaches of Anglo-American Treaties*,
> 1917

It was Great Britain's policy that inevitably led to the world war of 1914. It was a reversion to the mercantile policy of violence of the seventeenth and eighteenth centuries—not, though, by means of better ships and better goods, but by means of violence and destruction did they attempt to eliminate the undesirable competition.

> G. von Schmoller, 1919 (*see* Coole and Potter,
> 1941)

Comrade Sylvia Pankhurst is a representative of the interests of hundreds of people who are oppressed by the British and other Capitalists. That is why she is subjected to white terror, deprived of liberty, etc.

> Lenin, 30.v.1920, *see V. I. Lenin: British Labour
> and British Imperialism*, 1969

The Englishmen's fear of the Channel tunnel is fear of themselves. Capitalist barbarism is stronger than civilisation.

> *ibid.*

No nation prepared the way for its commercial conquests more brutally than England did by means of the sword and no other nation has defended such conquests more ruthlessly.

> A. Hitler, *Mein Kampf*, 1923 (transl. J. Murphy,
> 1939)

The traditional tendency of British diplomacy ever since the reign of Queen Elizabeth has been to employ systematically every possible means to prevent any one Power from attaining a preponderant position over the other European Powers and, if necessary, to break that preponderance by means of armed intervention. . . . The more difficult England's position became in the course of history, the more the British Imperial Government considered it necessary to maintain a condition of political paralysis among the various European States, as a result of their mutual rivalries. When the North American colonies obtained their political independence it became still more necessary for England to use every effort to establish and maintain the defence of her flank in Europe. In accordance with this policy she reduced Spain and the Netherlands to the position of inferior naval Powers. Having accomplished this, England concentrated all her forces against the increasing strength of France, until she brought about the downfall of Napoleon Bonaparte and therewith destroyed the military hegemony of France, which was the most dangerous rival that England had to fear.

ibid.

The English have always talked of freedom. They always sought their own freedom at the expense of everyone else's. They early developed a peculiar mode of thought based on a confusion of ideas, which gave precedence not to a cause for its own sake but to the advantage they themselves derived from it. There was no hypocrisy in this: though it looked like hypocrisy. It was merely an incredible *naïveté* combined with a natural brutality of approach. The English were perfectly unconscious of these things. Their trump card was their stupidity, and in their stupidity lay their highest shrewdness.

A. Moeller van den Bruck, *Das dritte Reich*, 1923
(transl. E. O. Lorimer, 1934)

The practical English mind was hard and pitiless. England has tolerated many encroachments on freedom; she tolerates truth only so long as society is not exposed. She is the land of the pauper and shuts her eyes to poverty and the uncleanness it brings in its train, so long as these things only affect strata of the population who constitute no danger to the state. The English liberals were credulous, well-meaning fellows, but fools: children who liked to cultivate illusions. When Bentham formulated his utilitarianism he genuinely deceived himself into thinking that self-interest, if only rightly understood, would lead to the welfare of all. A certain slovenliness pervades liberal thought: everything is good if it can be termed 'free' and twice good if it can be called 'useful' as well. Bentham interpreted the psychology of English utilitarianism fairly exactly when he explained duty, conscience and unselfishness on a basis of man's self-interest and claimed for his own doctrine that it aimed at 'regulating egotism'.

ibid.

There is an anecdote told of a British admiral, who, running into a bay that he had never seen before, dipped his finger into the water and, tasting it, said, 'Salt water. English territory.'

A. von Tirpitz, *Der Aubau der deutschen Weltmacht*, 1924

Poor, miserable, silly Fabianism, ignominious in its intellectual difficulties.

L. Trotsky, *Where is Britain Going?*, 1926

But the proletariat is held in check by just these groups who are their directing upper circles, in other words, by the Fabian politicians and their choral accompaniments. These bombastic authorities, pedants, arrogant and ranting poltroons, systematically poison the Labour Movement, befog the consciousness of the proletariat, and paralyse its will.

ibid.

And all the discussion of the question [political levies] in which the vital interests of two warring classes intersected, was carried on in this tone of conventionality, mental reservations, official double-dealing, purely British parliamentary cant. The reservations of the Conservatives have a Machiavellian character; the reservations of the Labour Party are the result of a contemptible cowardice. The bourgeois representation is similar to a tiger which sheathes its claws and pleasantly droops its eyelids; the labour leaders, such as Thomas, are like a beaten dog which puts its tail between its legs.

ibid.

The British bourgeoisie has been brought up on ruthlessness. The conditions of island existence, the moral philosophy of Calvinism, colonial practices, and national arrogance have led them along that road.

ibid.

The big boy appears as a lonely soul seeking companionship of good men and true and seeking with them a career in good works but finding always that they are crooks, rats, skunks, liars and hirelings of King George.[1] Does the big boy draw a friend to his bosom and he finds that he has admitted to his confidence a boodler, left-handed Irishman, snake, Swede, beer runner, polecat, Britisher, wart hog, sap, yegg, crook, rat, skunk, liar and hireling of King George.

Chicago Tribune, 19.iii.1927. Leader on
Mayor Thompson's election campaign

King George is probably running a fever by now knowing that our Bill will get him yet. When the big boy gets his spirit up it will be useless to double the guards at Buckingham Palace. More work for the undertaker, another little job for the casket maker, poor old England. Bill will make it in two jumps and come back with the crown jewels out of the Tower, some slabs of Westminster, Baldwin's high hat, the coronation robes, a trunkful of red robes, a fistful of monocles, the back hair of three or four peers, and the king's Sunday coat.

That will teach King George not to try his stuff in Chicago again, and if it shouldn't, Caesar had his Brutus, Charles I his Cromwell, and George V may profit by their example. If that be tommy rot, make the most of it.

Chicago Tribune, 25.iii.1927, Leader

The Englishman lives through different functions than ours.

---

[1] When asked whether he meant George V or George III, the Mayor is alleged to have replied: 'Good God! Are there two of them?'

He is the animal-man. At the lowest end of the scale he is the horse-man, with corresponding equine features . . .; at the highest end the Englishman is the ideal model of the political animal. In political matters, therefore, he is as much at home as a setter among partridges. For it is exactly thus that he understands politics, and not as a thinking person.

H. Keyserling, Europe, 1928 (transl. M. Samuel)

Thus she exacted tribute from the rest of the world. She grew rich. She put her profits back into world investments, and into a navy to perpetuate her holdings and her power. Whenever a serious competitor arose, she eliminated that competitor by war. Germany was not the first—and may not be the last.

L. Denny, America Conquers Britain, 1930

With biting scorn, the British poet [Rudyard Kipling] depicted Uncle Sam as going into the war at the eleventh hour and roughly shouldering aside the wearied soldiers already in the field.

More astonishing still, the Americans are described as 'swiftly' taking for their own the 'last spoils' of the war from the worn-out Britons.

It is not too much to say that the hatred and rancour of the poem left the Americans who read it almost breathless.

Doubtless there were many answers, but nobody answered it more good-naturedly than H. I. Phillips of the New York *Sun* in the following parody:

THE APPLESAUCE ORCHARD
(A reply to Rudyard Kipling's 'The Vineyard')

I

At the eleventh hour we came,
Late, perhaps, but pretty game;
Up they leap'd with shouts of joy,
And lusty cries of 'Attaboy!'

II

Since our backs had felt no load,
Eagerness in us abode;

And it's only fair to state,
No one said, 'Go home; you're late!'

III

Then they called us dearest brother—
Talked about our common mother;
Told in tears how much they'd missed us—
Hugged us, necked us . . . even kissed us!

IV

Then they called us 'noble chap',
'Pal' and 'hero'—all such pap;
Said our motives were the best—
Pinned big medals on our chest.

V

Then they went home, delivered hence,
Grudging us no recompense—
But (let's tell a truthful story)
They got all the territory.

VI

Rudyard, make some frank confessions:
England got the choice possessions;
Uncle Sam fulfilled a mission—
ALL HE GOT WAS PROHIBITION.

> G. H. Payne, *England: Her Treatment of America,*
> 1931 (quoting New York *Sun,* 2.ix.1927)

No idea is more deeply engrained in the British mind than that England must rule THE SEAS. Only those who are extremely gullible by inclination or by reason of lack of knowledge have taken seriously the recent declarations of modesty and the apparent renunciation of her position of Mistress of the Seas. To understand the Pacific problems we must remember that trade rivals are naval rivals. England has long held that a trade rival must in time be fought and put down.

England cares little who wins—she must be on the side of the conqueror—she must win a victory by defeat of either country. Even a stalemate will serve her purposes. The difficulties of her position are many. She has shrewdly and secretly cultivated Japanese goodwill and, artfully encouraging Japan in her dream of control of the Pacific, has been the main factor in encouraging Japan to become a bitter enemy of the United States, when once Japan was America's most devoted and grateful friend.

ibid.

PALMERSTON, THE TWO-BOTTLE MAN

Canning the Crafty was succeeded by Palmerston the Bold in the panorama of England's aggression against the United States. Where Canning had to tread softly by reason of the fact that he was a newcomer, a parvenu in the eyes of the governmental oligarchy, Palmerston, by reason of the fact that he was a mighty lord of aristocratic lineage, struck out right and left, regardless of the sensibilities of other nations, indifferent to right and wrong. Where Canning used brains to accomplish England's ends, Palmerston used bluster. '*Civis Romanus sum*, I am an Englishman,' he declared in Parliament in a speech that saved his bacon when he was on the verge of defeat, and that was hailed by his party as one of the great speeches of the century.

'I am an Englishman'—that was the national answer as expressed by Palmerston to the aggrieved and insulted of all nations, and if you didn't like it, you could lump it.

ibid.

The peace of the world may be insured by England and America, but only if England is rid of the carbuncles of two hundred and fifty years of selfishness.

ibid.

We confess that it gives us pleasure to meditate on the destruction that must sooner or later overtake this proud and seemingly invincible nation, and to think that this country, which was last conquered in 1066, will once more obey a foreign master, or at any rate have to resign its rich colonial empire.

E. Banse, *Raum und Volk im Weltkriege*, 1932
(transl. Alan Harris as *Germany, Prepare for War!*, 1934)

In the middle of the seventeenth century the bourgeois revolution in England developed under the guise of a religious reformation. A struggle for the right to pray according to one's own prayer book was identified with the struggle against the king, the aristocracy, the princes of the church, and Rome. The Presbyterians and Puritans were deeply convinced that they were placing their earthly interests under the unshakeable protection of the divine Providence. The goals for which the new classes were struggling commingled inseparably in their consciousness with texts from the Bible and the forms of churchly ritual. Emigrants carried with them across the ocean this tradition sealed with blood. Hence the extraordinary virility of the Anglo-Saxon interpretation of Christianity. We see even today how the minister 'socialists' of Great Britain back up their cowardice with these same magic texts with which the people of the seventeenth century sought to justify their courage.

L. Trotsky, *History of the Russian Revolution*
(transl. M. Eastman), 1934

England warmed up slowly. In the drawing-rooms of Petrograd and the head-quarters at the front they gently joked: 'England has sworn to fight to the last drop of blood . . . of the Russian soldier.'

ibid.

But England had, at any rate, ages at her disposal. She was the pioneer of bourgeois civilisation; she was not under the yoke of other nations, but on the contrary held them more and more under her yoke. She exploited the whole world. This softened the inner contradictions, accumulated conservatism, promoted an abundance and stability of fatty deposits in the form of a parasitic caste, in the form of a squirearchy, a monarchy, House of Lords, and the state church. Thanks to this exclusive historic privilege of development possessed by bourgeois England, conservatism combined with elasticity passed over from her institutions into her moral fibre. Various continental Philistines, like the Russian professor Miliukov, or the Austro-Marxist Otto Bauer, have not to this day ceased going into ecstasies over this fact. But exactly at the present moment, when England, hard pressed throughout the world, is squandering the last resources of her former privileged position, her conservatism is losing its elasticity, and even in the person of the Labourites is turning into stark reactionism. In the face of the Indian revolution the 'socialist' MacDonald will find no other methods but those with which Nicholas II opposed the Russian revolution. Only a blind man could fail to see that Britain is headed for gigantic revolutionary earthquake shocks, in which the last fragments of her conservatism, her world domination, her present state machine, will go down without a trace.

ibid.

Listen, John Bull: The traditional principle of your politics, the unique driving force of your behaviour, the doctrine professed always by your publicists and orators and practised by your statesmen, is purely self-interest. It is impossible to recall all the notorious examples of violence, perfidy, implacable egoism, and disloyalty with which your national history is sullied. Stirring up nations, fomenting internal dissensions in other countries in order to exhaust them, sowing discord between nations, and profiting by all these conflicts in order to achieve some new conquest, arming peoples in the cause of their national independence, then abandoning them mercilessly, hiring traitors, crushing, expropriating, decimating conquered races—all these acts abound in your annals; you have never looked upon them except as legitimate manifestations of your right and it is with sincerity that you have always known how to subordinate ethical principles to that sacred trust that you call English interests. Justice, humanity, the liberty of nations, peace and war, are treated by you as matters of finance. You who hold such an important place in the world, quote me in the history of your foreign policy one single act of devotion, of spontaneous enthusiasm, one single disinterested act. There is no nation on earth which has not been a victim of your arrogance, your cruelty, your greed, your perfidy, Britannic faith.

H. Béraud, *Faut-il réduire l'Angleterre en esclavage?*, 1935

John Bull's method of conducting his foreign affairs, when his own major interests have not directly been affected, and even when he has been acting in concert with another power against a common enemy, has always been to let someone else bear the brunt, while he himself, all unconcerned, has avoided making any sacrifices.

T. Ishimaru, Japan must fight Britain (transl.
G. V. Rayment), 1936

England, by defeating her competitors on the sea one after the other, gained the mastery of the world and brought vast tracts of it under her sway. To retain these in peace and safety it has been essential for her to prevent the rise of more than one other Power at the same time. This necessity has been the basis of her traditional policy on the Continent of Europe, and was the reason why she endeavoured to nip in the bud Germany's challenge to her supremacy. Her policy in Asia has been precisely the same, and Japan has the honour (?) for receiving her attentions in this respect. England knew what she was doing when she made the Anglo-Japanese Alliance. She had already devised a means of keeping Japanese expansion within definite limits.

ibid.

The English might come into an American-Japanese war if they thought that by the exercise of their cunning diplomacy, and by waiting until both belligerents were worn out, they could become Masters of the World without taking their hands out of their pockets.

ibid.

There was something fascinating about the British approach to the Indian problem, even though it was singularly irritating. The calm assurance of always being in the right and of having borne a great burden worthily, faith in their racial destiny and their own brand of imperialism, contempt and anger at the unbelievers and sinners who challenged the foundations of the true faith—there was something of the religious temper about this attitude. Like the Inquisitors of old, they were bent on saving us regardless of our desires in the matter.

Jawaharlal Nehru, *An Autobiography*, 1936

More interesting is the comparison of England with Austria, for has not England of the twentieth century been compared to Austria of the nineteenth, proud and haughty and imposing still, but with the roots that gave strength shrivelling up and decay eating its way into the mighty fabric.

ibid.

In the House of Commons the rulers of Britain maintain the world's most exclusive and powerful club.

Quincy Howe, *England Expects every American to do his Duty*, 1938

The history of Anglo-American relations might seem, on the surface, to suggest that British statesmen had bludgeoned or bamboozled American statesmen into taking orders from Downing Street. But the power that Britain wields in the United States does not arise from intellectual or economic superiority. If England, in its hour of need, expects every American to do his duty, that expectation does not arise from the usual economic considerations. On the contrary. If material factors alone determined American national policy, the United States would either have taken over the British Empire after the war or retired into its shell. Instead, it has puttered about the four corners of the earth, only to emerge at every critical juncture defending British interests more heartily than the British themselves.

ibid.

The British were a brave people, but they did not like to fight themselves. They preferred to fight to the last Frenchman, as in the World War, or, as recently, to the last Abyssinian, and now to the last Chinese.

Adolf Hitler, Conversation with Stoyadinovich, 17.i.1938 (*Docs. on Ger. For. Pol.*, D.V.163)

Damn it all, tradition has to be kept up—the tradition of an empire built upon blood, injustice, treaty-breaking and savagery!

> *B. Z. Am Mittag*, 22.iii.1939 (*see* W. G. Knop,
> *Beware of the English*, 1939)

The British lion has grown old. He lies sated, with greying whiskers, grasping his prey with all four paws. . . . His teeth are gradually growing loose, while his paws, how embarrassing, show traces of gout. Then, too, his hearing is no longer good, and a film is spreading over his tired eyes.

> *N. S. Kurier*, 29.iii.1939 (*ibid.*)

For 300 years this England has acted only as the least virtuous of nations in order now in her old age to talk of virtue! Thus it was that in this period when England was not virtuous 46 millions of English folk conquered almost a quarter of the world, while 86 million Germans because of their virtue had to live 140 to the square kilometer.

Yes, and only twenty years ago the question of virtue was still not completely cleared up for British statesmen so far as ideas of property were concerned. At that time it was still thought to be compatible with virtue simply to take from other people the colonies which that people had acquired only through treaties or purchase—because one had power to do so—that power which today, certainly, is to be regarded as abominable, a thing deserving nothing save men's abomination.

> Adolf Hitler, speech in front of Wilhelmshafen
> Rathaus, 1.iv.1939 (*see* N. Baynes, *The Speeches*
> *of Adolf Hitler*, 1942)

Who bears the blame for the Polish war?	England!
Who preaches murder from old to young?	England!
Who tramples on the rights of neutrals?	England!
Who makes the innocent suffer for the guilty?	England!

> England, the curse of all the world,
> Thrives on greed, hate and gold.

Who feigns love and sows only hate?	England!
Who gave Polish murderers their charter?	England!

Who robbed children of father and mother?	England!
Who was counsellor to the murderers in Poland?	England!

England, the curse of all the world,
Thrives on greed, hate and gold.

Who causes nations to bleed to death?	England!
Who is the friend of traitors and Jews?	England!
Who keeps nations in bondage and slavery?	England!
Who makes parents and children starve?	England!

England, the curse of all the world,
Thrives on greed, hate and gold.

Who torpedoes its own ships?	England!
Who is a master of lies and tricks?	England!
Who shoots down even Belgian 'planes?	England!
Who has refused to return our colonies?	England!

England, the curse of all the world,
Thrives on greed, hate and gold.

Paul Kirchhoff, October, 1939[1] (*see Der Stürmer*,
no. 40)

When England clashes with another power, not only does blood flow, but the Britisher defiles himself with deeds of bestial brutality that would make any other nation blush with shame.

E. Schultze, *Die Blutspur Englands*, 1940

No nation has committed a greater number of atrocities, no nation has shown baser traits therein;—and no other nation has tried, in spite of them, or indeed with reference to them, to set up its lofty ethical notions as a shining example to all the world. This hypocrisy makes of the English atrocities a phenomenon, the vileness of which is only surpassed by its treachery.

ibid.

With true English cynicism, they have treacherously forsaken their friends.

Ribbentrop to Stalin, 13.x.1940 (*Docs. on Ger.
For. Pol.*, D. XI)

[1] This new Hymn of Hate by an Aryan was commissioned by the Nazis, as Lissauer's famous *Hassgesang* of the 1914–18 war was composed by a Jew.

England, that relentless and crafty enemy of the true liberties of peoples, has never tired of forging chains to enslave and subjugate the Arab people, sometimes in the name of a perfidious League of Nations and sometimes by flaunting false and hypocritical sentiments of humanity for the others, but always, in truth, for the most imperialistic designs camouflaged by the principles of democracy and of a mendacious internationalism.

> Mohammed Amin El Husseini, Grand Mufti of
> Palestine, Baghdad, to A. Hitler, 20.i.1941
> (*ibid.* D.XI, 1151)

The English people seem to me to be rather constipated. Things must come to a pretty bad pass before they lose their nerve. We must handle them much more carefully. The German people remind us even today of careless turns of speech used during the first weeks of the war. They have a good memory in that regard. The English sometimes give you the impression that they haven't any memory at all.

> Joseph Goebbels, *Diary*, 25.ii.1942
> (L. P. Lochner, *The Goebbels Diaries*, 1948)

A typically English thing is happening in London in that a prayer racket for India has been scheduled. The bishops and priests have been mobilised for it. They are to address fervent prayers to God to let the Indians have the food that the English have stolen from them.

> *ibid.*, 30.xi.1943

So the English are fighting to be free and at the same time fighting the Indians who are fighting to be free, and the Indians are fighting to be free in order to help the English fighting to be free in this war of freedom. This has become such a confounded mess that if the Englishman in India ever thinks, he ought to die of apoplexy. I have no fear that he will. One just does not discuss the Four Freedoms in India, nor hear them mentioned. It is a little awkward, isn't it? Win the war first and use your brains afterwards. Only a robust English mind can survive these logical inconsistencies, and I have no doubt it will. You are sure of it when you hear the tone of satisfaction in the Viceroy of India's report on killings in India: 940 killed, 1,630 injured, 60,229 arrested, 26,000 convicted, 18,000 detained without trial—since August, 1942. As a correspondent in the *New Republic* puts it: 'the Viceroy reports it like so many stuck hogs on a line in a Chicago packing-house.' Every one of these hogs is a fighter for freedom, and not afraid to be beaten, flogged, or sent to jail for it. A hog is a hog, or ain't it?

Lin Yutang, Between Tears and Laughter, 1945

From my college days, I have heard of the 'white man's burden' and have often wondered what is inside that knapsack which the white man carries on his back around the globe. I have now discovered that it is only canned goods. Poor Kipling, he would not have remained alive and returned to be Lord Rector of St Andrews if he were deprived during his stay in India of corned beef and sardines. Still you cannot deny that he successfully converted corned beef and sardines into some good rousing verse, breathing pluck and faith in a so very enlightened scheme of shipping that made corned beef obtainable in faraway Allahabad and Lahore.

ibid.

I wonder sometimes why the English royal family lets anyone who might come to the throne lets him be called George how can they, to be sure Shakespeare said a rose will smell as sweet by any name but will it. No it will not. Consider the name George. Every time there was a George on the throne there was trouble bad trouble. The first two Georges gradually reduced England from the glory that Anne and Marlborough following William and Mary had given them, and then came George III and all misfortune, did he not lose colonies and go mad and then George the fourth and the first world war, with Napoleon and then no more Georges for a bit, and then after Victoria and Edward and Edward would not have a world war came George V a nice man but with all the misfortunes of a world war and then an Edward, would the world war have come had Edward stayed on but he did not, not, and a George came and bang a world war once again and plenty of misfortune and so will they again will the royal family again have the temerity to call a son who might come to the throne George. Better not, really better not. There is something in a name all the same.

Gertrude Stein, *Wars I have Seen*, 1945

Nothing is more menacing to British imperialism than an awakening of colonial peoples and an increase in their living standards. So long as the subjected peoples are kept down, the empire can stay up. For otherwise, what need would non-British peoples have for British rulers?

Saul K. Padover in *P.M.*, 21.viii.1946

Palestine, administered by the British along purely fascist lines, complete with total censorship, arbitrary curfews, concentration camps, filled prisons, and police brutality.

ibid.

One trouble with the British is that our bond of sympathy with them is so close that they know they can take advantage of us. Like an old man with a weakness for going on benders, the British know that when they get into trouble, their indulgent son will always bail them out.

Drew Pearson, in *Washington Post*, 22.viii.1946

The terms of international relations have been largely invented by the Anglo-Saxon powers. Years ago Britain compiled a great dictionary of moral words by which she accumulated an empire. Today she has modernised the vocabulary so that whatever is required by the logic of her foreign policy, whether the suppression of revolts or the massing of troops on foreign borders, she manages with dignity and a minimum loss of prestige.

H. Lamont, Jr., *ibid.*, 22.viii.1946

My dear General
    The skill of our enemy (England)
in forging false news . . . annual custom to
    send out these cargoes of lies it is
    their way of passing the winter
thus by 'appeasing the troubles in Ireland'
    by contracts with German princes
and especially Petersburg: 20,000 russians
                    12 ships of the line
              also Denmark 45 vessels (line)
(to La Fayette and to Genet)
'the art of political lying in England better than elsewhere'
19th (next day)
    'no contracts with German princes'
                Ezra Pound, *Seventy Cantos*, LXVIII, 1950

Gone are the times when the British lion roared and everything trembled. Now it can frighten no-one.
          N. Khrushchev, 30.iv.1958, quoted in *The Times*,
                    1.v.1958

Unite to save Kuwait from the jaws of the British Lion.
          Damascus newspaper, 10.vii.1961

Great Britain has lost an empire and has not yet found a role.
          Dean Acheson, 5.xii.1962

Next year Britain will become a fourth-rate country and later a fifth-rate one.
          President Nasser, 23.xii.1962, in Victory Square,
          Port Said, reported in *The Times*, 24.xii.1962

Index

P